Success to the Lace Pillow

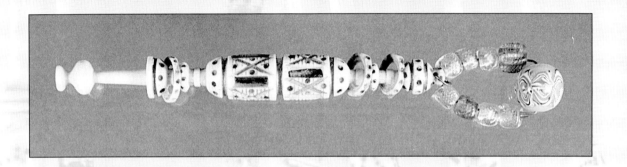

*The Classification and Identification
of 19th Century East Midland
Lace Bobbins and Their Makers.*

By
Christine & David Springett

This book is for Beach and Margaret
for their support over many years. With thanks.

Acknowledgements

We would like to thank the following people for the help they have given us during our research.

Bridget Cook, Sylvia Chandler, Mary Cruwys, Yvonne Curtis, John & Eva Cummings, Victor Hatley, Stella Herbert, Vivien Heywood, Miss Hueman, Stuart King, Mrs E. Knight, Mr & Mrs Mayes, Sue Morris, Pauline Robinson, Diana Smith, Geraldine Stott & Ruth Wyke.

The Editor of 'The Bedford Times' and the Editor of 'The Independent' newspapers.

The archivist of The House of Commons. The staff of Buckinghamshire, Bedfordshire & Northamptonshire County Record Offices.

Miss Ewles, the then keeper of social history, Aylesbury Museum. Sylvia Crawley of Buckinghamshire County Museum. Mr J. Turner, the then Curator of Bedford Museum. Rosemary Brind, Curator of Bedford Museum. Judith Hodgkinson of Northampton Museum. Doreen Fudge, the then Curator of Luton Museum.

Museums with collections of lace bobbins

Birmingham Museum and Art Gallery.

Bedford Museum.

Buckinghamshire County Museum, Aylesbury.

Cecil Higgins Art Gallery, Bedford.

Cowper and Newton Museum, Olney.

Luton Museum.

Northampton Museum. (By appointment).

Victoria and Albert Museum.

First published in 1997 by

C & D Springett

21, Hillmorton road,

Rugby,

Warwickshire.

CV22 5DF.

© C & D Springett 1997.

ISBN 0 9517157 5 5

Illustrations By Tim Benké and Robin Springett.

All rights reserved.

Printed by Neil Terry Printing, Rugby 568000.

Contents

Introduction 1

Methods of identification 1

Dating bobbins 3

Glossary of terms 4

The bobbin maker's workshop 5

Election bobbins 8

Hanging bobbins 13

Trade bobbins 17

Queen Caroline 18

Religious inscriptions 19

"Music Hall" inscriptions 20

The "Bitted" man 21

Jesse and James Compton 23

    Jesse Compton 23

    James Compton 27

Joseph, David and Robert Haskins 30

    Joseph Haskins 32

    David Haskins 37

    Robert Haskins 40

William "Bobbin" Brown 41

Arthur Wright 46

The "Blunt end" man 48

Archibald Abbott. 52

Bobbin maker No. 1 55

Bobbin maker No. 2 56

Bobbin maker No. 3 57

Bobbin maker No. 4 58

The Saunders brothers of Waddesdon 59

Early 20th century bobbins 61

    (1) J. Harris 61

    (2) E.P. Rose 64

    (3) 1920's and 30's bobbins 67

    (4) Les Green 68

Other known makers 68

Oddities 69

Bobbins from other parts of Britain. 75

    South Bucks. bobbins 75

    Devon bobbins 76

    Downton bobbins 77

    Malmesbury bobbins 77

Materials used in bobbin making 78

Lace tokens 83

"Caveat emptor" 85

Heads and tails at a glance 89

Bibliography 92

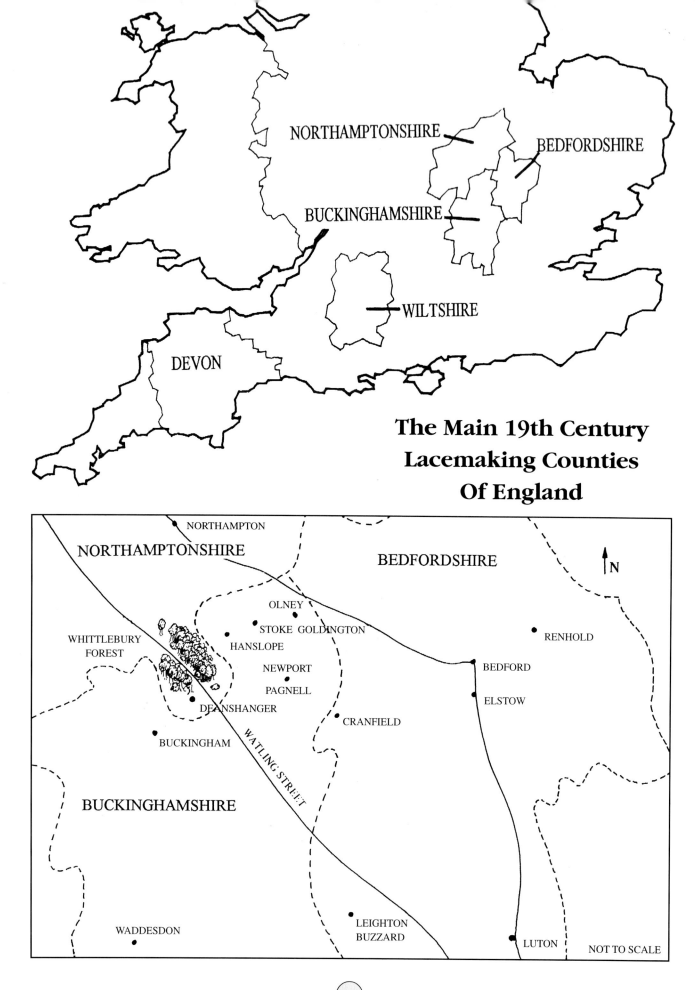

NORTHAMPTONSHIRE

BEDFORDSHIRE

BUCKINGHAMSHIRE

WILTSHIRE

DEVON

The Main 19th Century
Lacemaking Counties
Of England

NORTHAMPTON

NORTHAMPTONSHIRE

BEDFORDSHIRE

N

OLNEY

STOKE GOLDINGTON

WHITTLEBURY
FOREST

HANSLOPE

RENHOLD

NEWPORT
PAGNELL

BEDFORD

ELSTOW

DEANSHANGER

CRANFIELD

BUCKINGHAM

WATLING STREET

BUCKINGHAMSHIRE

WADDESDON

LEIGHTON
BUZZARD

LUTON

NOT TO SCALE

A selection of bobbins made by Archibald Abbott.
Bone and wood dyed bobbins, pewter inlaid tigers and butterflies, mother and babe, screwthread decoration and
two inscribed bobbins – "Hannah Abbott" on bone and "Fear God" on boxwood.

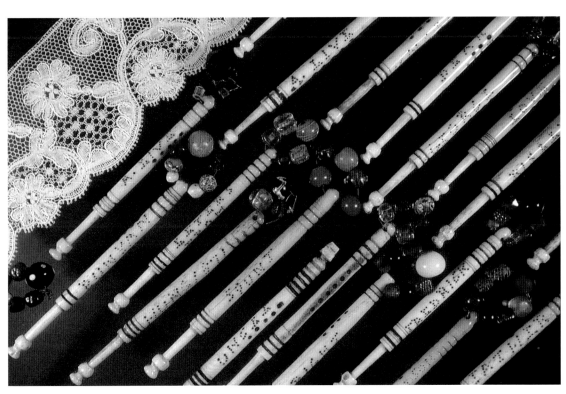

The 'Blunt End' man inscriptions from left to right.
Bottom staggered line, "Jack A Live", "John Bunyan", "A Gift from Leters", W. Bull Hung 1871", "SQUNT WLTE", "Uncle Daniel",
reverse of a poor piece of bone, "Rosera Right", "Fredrick".
Top line, "Jack A Live", "Uncle Joel", "Dear Daniel", "Dear George", "God Is Love", "Charles Risely".

Bobbins made by Jesse and James Compton.
Inscriptions read – (from left to right) – Bone with spirals of beads, "When This You See Remember Me. J. Roberts", "Aunt Smith Died Padbury Nov 9 1875", "FRANK", "ROB ♡", "Wakes Oak", "When This You See Remember Me And Bear Me In Your Mind Let All The World Say What Thay Will, Speek Of Me As You Find 26 MAY 1841", "Respect The Giver J S 1836", Bone Pewter inlaid with dyed bistre coloured head and initial "B" inscribed, "Robinson For Ever", "FANNY", "James Compton Mary Ann Compton 1841", a bone pen handle (above), "Thomas Chappell Aged 20 years", "A Present From J.S. 1838".

A variety of bobbins made by the "Bitted" man.
Inscribed on the bottom line from left to right – Bone "John Weer May 25 1815", bone pewter inlay with the initials "B C", wood thorn inlay initials "M R", bone inscription "Love And Live Happy", wood thorn inlay initials "E R", bone inscription "Love me CP". Top line; bone inscribed "M A W", wood thorn inlay initials "A R".

Bobbins by William 'Bobbin' Brown and Arthur Wright (underlined).
Inscriptions reading from right to left, bottom row.
"Slap Bang Here We Go Again", "William Lawson My Father A D Oct 12 1853", "W. Worsley Hung 1868".
"Don't Be Absent", a bone pewter inlaid, a wood mother and babe, "Mary Lawson My Mother Died Dec. 31 1853",
"Love Don't You List", "Love Is True In Bedfordshire ♡", and a wood pewter inlaid butterfly.

A variety of bobbins made by Joseph, Robert and David Haskins.

"Oddities".
From left to right.
A glass bobbin, whittled wood bobbin, a Jesse Compton pewter inlaid bone bobbin with a bead shank, a splendid brass "Birdcage"
mother and babe, a devon bobbin which reads, "Let Virtue Be A Gaide To Thee E.M., R.H. 1816".
A french post card, a bronze plaquette and lace tokens.

A group of unusual bobbins from right to left.
Inlaid Windmills, Pewter trolley bobbin inscribed "Kis Me If You Will My Love And Kis Me In The Park 1847", bone Porthole bobbin,
brass bobbin inscribed "John Wesley", bone inscribed "Henry Wall Pereira", Pewter mother and babe, Election bobbin "Lord Milton",
bone inscribed "Reckles", bone with spliced head and neck inscribed "David", a bone Mother and babe, and a beaded shank bobbin.

Introduction

As bobbin makers of the present day, we draw heavily on the styles and designs used by bobbin makers during the previous two centuries. It was inevitable that our fascination with these old bobbins should lead us to a closer investigation of the craftsmen responsible for producing them.

It has not been easy to discover precisely which bobbins were made by a certain craftsman, as this was not considered to be a subject of sufficient importance to merit detailed written description at the time when bobbin making was commonplace. Later records give us tantalising glimpses of the bobbin makers techniques in such general terms that they are of little practical help in positively identifying the work of a specific bobbin maker.

Later records give us

tantalising glimpses of the

bobbin makers techniques

Much valuable information has been passed down by word of mouth, but as the men who made their living making bobbins probably died the best part of one hundred years ago, accurate details are very hard to come by. Our attempts to contact descendants of past bobbin makers, who might have been able to recognize bobbins made by their grandfather or great uncle, have unfortunately met with no success. We have spoken to old lacemakers and asked if they can remember a local bobbin maker, but the few bobbins they needed to buy were always purchased from a shop — most frequently the shop where they bought their thread and sold their finished lace.

Most craftsmen developed a characteristic style of bobbin, the shaping of the head, tail or shank allowing us to distinguish between one bobbin maker's work and another. On looking through the extensive collections of bobbins, both in museums and those in private ownership, it is easy to spot the bobbins which have been made by one individual. We have concentrated our attention on those bobbin makers whose bobbins we found in the greatest numbers. A great many lace bobbins have not survived the years in which the handmade lace industry fell into decline, so it is reasonable to assume that where a large number of a certain maker's bobbins have survived, it is probably because he made a greater number of bobbins in the first place. This would perhaps indicate the more successful and popular makers of the time rather than the husband or lover who just made a few bobbins for his wife or sweetheart. We have also found that some of these very prolific makers produced some outstandingly splendid and eye-catching designs.

In the fifteen years since 1981 when we published the first edition of "Success to the Lace Pillow", (our original booklet about antique bobbins) we have seen and studied thousands more bobbins. The information we have gathered in that time has been added to the original text where appropriate, and in some instances new sections have been created. Sadly it is still not possible to confidently put names to the makers of some of the groups of bobbins we have identified and despite our research we have still to discover which bobbins were made by some of the bobbin makers referred to in Thomas Wright's "The Romance Of The Lace Pillow" so our criterion for selecting this `elite' of bobbin makers has been a combination of the two factors, quality and quantity.

We hope that in producing this book you will not only be able to learn a little more about the antique bobbins in your possession, but that it may also inspire the reader to contact us with any additional facts or opinions which would help to make our future efforts more accurate and more interesting. So much valuable information has already been lost, that we feel it is very important that every effort should be made to collect together even the smallest snippets of information, which would be of great interest to the ever increasing number of lacemakers throughout the country and the world.

Methods Of Identification

In the same way that one person's handwriting is different from that of his neighbour, so one maker's bobbins will be different from those produced by another bobbin maker, and it is not difficult to develop an "eye" for the distinctive features which are the hallmark of a particular craftsman's work.

The tools a man uses, and the way in which he uses them, leads him to evolve a shape of head, neck or tail, which remains remarkably constant. There may be minor deviations from day to day, but as with handwriting, the basic style is always the same. So a close examination of the size, shape and proportion of the different parts of the bobbin is one of the most important pointers towards identifying the bobbins made by one man.

The second important feature for the purposes of identification is the style of decoration employed by the bobbin maker. This may be in the form of lettering or in the addition of beads, wire, tinsel, pewter and coloured bands, slashes or spots, but again the makers producing a large number of bobbins tended to use such decoration in their own characteristic way.

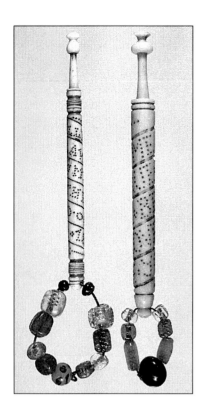

Pewter inlay can also help distinguish between the work of one turner and another. The Archibald Abbott pewter inlaid Butterfly on the left of the photograph points towards the right, but the Bobbin Brown pewter inlaid Butterfly next to it, points to the left. Different workers worked in different ways.

◄ *Fig. 1.1*
Right (on right) and Left Hand spiral (on left).

Bobbin Brown of Cranfield

was left handed and always cut

a left hand spiral

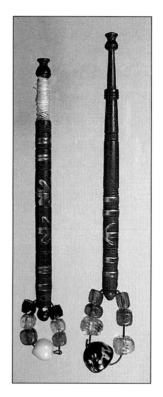

It is important that a number of similar features are identified before stating that certain bobbins were made by the same craftsman. It is not enough that they should both have lettering in red, or similar arrangements of coloured bands. There should really be a combination of similar characteristics involving both shape and decorative details. We have tried to set ourselves very strict standards when attributing a bobbin, or group of bobbins to a certain maker, and if we have felt that there has been room for doubt, then we have not included them. It may be that at some point in the future we shall find "the missing link" which convincingly relates one group of bobbins to another, and which will allow us to confidently attribute both groups to the same maker or as in the case of the three generations of bobbin makers in the Haskins family, further refine our original identification enabling us to distinguish between each man's work.

The formation of the individual letters or numbers on inscribed bobbins gives a very clear indication of those which were made by the same hand. The colour of the lettering, the arrangement of coloured bands, or the spots or slashes on the reverse side of a named bobbin, may confirm that the bobbin originated from the same workshop.

The spiral line cut upon a bobbin either for wire decoration or for a spiral inscription is an important indicator. Bobbin Brown of Cranfield was left handed and always cut a left hand spiral, whereas James Compton of Deanshanger was right handed and always cut a right hand spiral. (See photograph above).

The two horizontally inscribed bobbins in the photograph below can be easily read — Martha and James — but note that to read the name Martha the head of the bobbin has to be on the left, whereas to read the name James the bobbin head has to be on the right. This is another important point to consider when comparing bobbins.

▲ *Fig. 1.3 Butterflies pointing different ways*

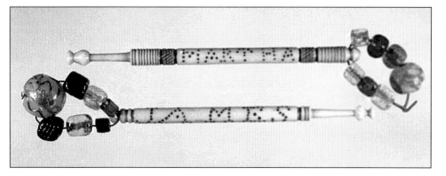

▲ *Fig. 1.2 'Martha' Head on the Left – 'James' Head on the Right*

Dating Bobbins

At first sight it appears very easy to date many bobbins which the maker has kindly inscribed with a name and a date, but just because a bobbin bears the date 1864, it does not necessarily follow that it was actually made in that year. As bobbin makers of today, we are frequently requested to inscribe bobbins with names and dates referring to family members who were born many years ago, and so it must have been with many commissions that previous bobbin makers received. Lacemakers have always been noted for their industry rather than their financial reward, and it may have taken some time for sufficient money to be saved before ordering a special bobbin to commemorate a particular birth or death. So it must be pointed out that many bobbins are not as old as the inscribed date suggests. However, as such commemorative bobbins could not have been ordered in advance, it is safe to say that neither are they older than the date they bear.

▲ *Fig. 1.4 A Buckinghamshire Lacemaker*

There is one category of inscriptions which probably gives a more accurate indication of when a bobbin was made and these are the so-called "hanging" bobbins made to commemorate the execution of several notorious murderers in the nineteenth century. These were made as souvenirs to be sold, or given away, on the day of the execution. There would have been little call to repeat the inscription a long time after the event, so it is reasonable to assume that such bobbins were made during that year.

A number of bobbins are inscribed with the names of political figures and were presumably commissioned by prospective MPs and given away to electors in an effort to secure their vote. Some of these can be more accurately dated than others. For instance the inscription "Gunning for Reform" was a clear reference to the Parliamentary Reform Bill of 1832, and is confirmed by the fact that Sir Robert Gunning sat for Northampton Borough from August 1830 until June 1831. Unfortunately we have no way of knowing whether Sir Robert distributed these favours as part of his successful campaign in 1830, or his unsuccessful campaign in 1831, but it does allow us to date the bobbin within a year of its making.

By closely examining "hanging" or "election" bobbins it may be possible to relate them to other bobbins with similar distinguishing features which could have been made by the same maker, and thus give some indication of when that maker was producing bobbins.

It is probably true to say

that very few decorative or inscribed

bobbins were made in the

traditional manner after 1890.

The ups and downs of the handmade lace industry during the nineteenth century must also have been reflected in the demand for, and production of, new lace bobbins. In the first half of the nineteenth century, when lacemakers enjoyed a period of comparatively greater prosperity, more people made lace, and far more bobbins would have been required than during the second half of the century when the handmade lace industry had tried, and failed, to compete with the cheaper machine-made lace. This can clearly be seen in the types of inscribed bobbins which were sold during the last century. For instance, a bobbin maker in the earlier years of the century found a ready sale for his bobbins and probably had a stock range of inscribed bobbins carrying such general sentiments as "If I love the boys tis nothing to nobody", but when times became harder during the third quarter of the nineteenth century there were far fewer of these general inscriptions, bobbin makers finding that the bobbins which he did sell, were mainly those ordered to commemorate a specific family event, and very few of these were dated later than the 1880's.

It is probably true to say that very few decorative or inscribed bobbins were made in the traditional manner after 1890. Most of the well known bobbin makers had died by this time, and the lack of demand for new bobbins did not encourage the sons to carry on their father's trade to any great degree and the skills of the bobbin maker, along with those of the lacemaker, fell into serious decline. So the vast majority of decorated and inscribed bobbins were made prior to 1890, and most that survive today, will be at least one hundred years old. We hope that the information and the photographs of bobbins on the following pages will help you to identify, and perhaps to date, some of your own bobbins.

Glossary of Terms

The types of decoration used on bobbins, and the various parts of a bobbin, are sometimes known by different names, therefore it is important to give a brief definition of the terms we have used so that no confusion arises.

The bobbin

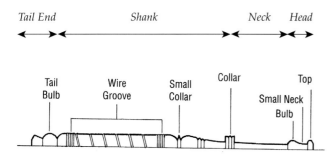

Types of decoration

Beaded: very fine beads threaded on wire which is wound around the shank, the beads being positioned in grooves to form a wide variety of patterns.

Bead shank: a number of glass beads mounted on thick wire to form part of the shank.

Bitted: inlaid with small pieces of wood, or occasionally bone.

Brass pinned: brass pins hammered into the shank and filed off flush to form letters or patterns.

Church window: shank decorated with empty pierced openings, it is said to have been inspired by the window pattern on Olney church spire.

Cow and calf: the end section of the hollow shank pulls out to reveal a miniature bobbin which is attached to the tail part.

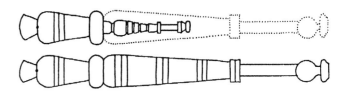

Dyed: at least part, or the whole bobbin having been immersed in dye.

Fairing: inlaid with tinsel (cut from thin sheets of metal, often coloured) in narrow grooves or in wide bands around the shank. The term used to apply to any gaudy item bought at a fair, or a present brought home from a fair. Many bobbin makers sold their bobbins at such events.

Inscribed: Named: names, dates or inscriptions written horizontally along the length of the shank.

Spiral inscription: inscription or name arranged spirally around the shank of the bobbin.

Spirals: whether they are cut to form part of the decoration on a bobbin or on a spirally inscribed bobbin, can be either right or left handed.

Right Handed

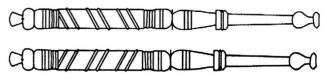

Left Handed

Jack in the box: two parts of the hollow shank pull apart to release a loose miniature bobbin.

Jingle: loose wooden, bone or pewter rings decorating the shank.

Lantern: small beads or shot enclosed in the compartment of a pierced shank.

Mother and babe: miniature bobbin or bobbins enclosed in a pierced shank.

Old maid: a very slim and plain bobbin.

Ornamentally turned: the shank is embellished with ridges, rounds and hollows.

Pewter inlay:

Butterfly: inlaid with pewter in the form of a butterfly, arrowhead or crows foot, sometimes called a Bedford — fly.

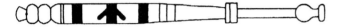

Leopard: inlaid with pewter spots.

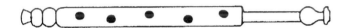

Tiger: inlaid with pewter bands around the shank.

Screwthread: a very tight spiral groove running up the shank.

Spot decoration:

Domino: a bone bobbin decorated with spots arranged in the same way as the spots on a domino.

Four penny spot: a bone bobbin decorated with four large spots arranged as illustrated below.

Thorn: thorns of a contrasting colour driven into the shank to form letters or a pattern.

Wired: bound with brass or copper wire.

The bobbin maker's workshop

The workshop of the bobbin maker two hundred years ago would have been a very different sight from that used by the bobbin maker today. Now we have circular saws, bandsaws, power drills, high speed lathes and a dozen other pieces of sophisticated machinery to make the bobbin maker's life as effortless as possible. It would be all too easy to take a rather scornful, or patronising view of the "primitive" tools used a century or two ago, but when you have closely studied

▲ *Stuart King, Artist, Craftsman.*
Demonstrating bobbin making at his treadle lathe.

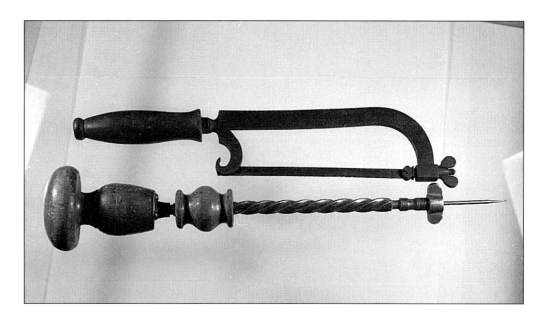

▲ *Fig 2.1 - 19th Century Hacksaw and Archimedian Drill*

the bobbins produced at that time, and have tried to produce similar bobbins, then a very different perspective is revealed. The old craftsmen might not have had such sophisticated

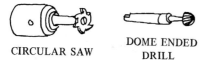

CIRCULAR SAW   DOME ENDED
                         DRILL

Fig 2.2

hardware at their disposal, but the tools which they had were more than adequate when used in a practised, skilful way.

The high speed electric lathe of today would probably have been regarded with an equal amount of wonder and suspicion. The bobbin maker of the last century would most likely have used a treadle lathe. This was of simple construction, and could have been made locally with the combined efforts of the village blacksmith, carpenter, wheelwright and harness maker.

The turning tools used on the lathe could also have been made by the local blacksmith, who was probably quite experienced in forging the good quality steel from such items as broken scythes, into very effective turning tools. Old files could also be sharpened and shaped to serve a variety of

purposes according to a bobbin maker's particular requirements.

The drill required to make the spots to form the lettering or decoration on the bobbins, was possibly an archimedian drill. This would have been available from the nearest town, or from the traveller who would frequently visit the local carpenter or wheelwright to supply all the tools and hardware sundries needed by such craftsmen. This drill is both accurate and easy to use and enabled some bobbin makers to achieve lettering of great neatness.

Specialised drill bits were also available. These were made by various firms who published catalogues and distributed them to hardware shops in the towns. More elaborate turning tools could also be bought from such suppliers if they were needed. A dome ended drill bit would have been ideal for making shallow dots and spots, no doubt the bobbin maker could have made his own simplified version of this fine drill. To cut the windows in a mother and babe bobbin the turner might well have taken a nail and filed teeth around its head to produce a circular saw type cutter. If the shank of the nail is held in the headstock of the lathe and the lathe treadled, a turned bobbin can be carefully lowered on to the rotating cutter thus cutting a slot. Further slots can be cut around the bobbin to form the open windows of a mother and babe. This may well sound rather crude to

▲ *Fig 2.3 Abbott Mother & Babe – Note the curved end of the window*

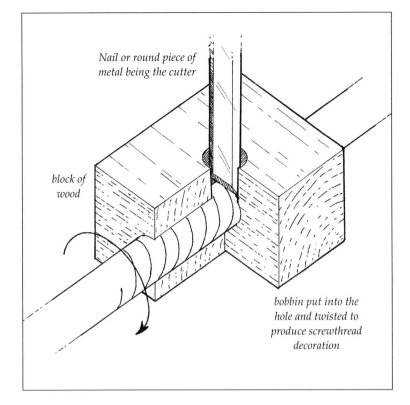

Nail or round piece of
metal being the cutter

block of
wood

bobbin put into the
hole and twisted to
produce screwthread
decoration

◄ Fig 2.4

Various saws would have been needed. Some were factory produced and purchased in the nearest town, like the small hacksaw shown in the photograph, which would certainly have been available throughout the nineteenth century. Others were probably made by the blacksmith, who would also have been able to satisfy any individual requirements of the bobbin maker.

It is quite likely that a number of very ingenious jigs and less conventional tools were used by some bobbin makers as they solved their own particular problems. For instance, many of the cheapest type of bobbins were decorated with a tight spiralling groove. It is very unlikely that bobbins bearing this screwthread were made on a special lathe as bobbin makers would not have been able to afford an expensive specialist screw cutting lathe.

We have experimented with various ideas in an effort to discover how this spiral might have been made, and we have found that a jig made in the following manner, is quite successful. A block of wood has a hole drilled through it, just wide enough to take the bobbin. A second, smaller hole is drilled to cross the first, and a metal rod, or even a nail which has been sharpened to a chisel point, is then pushed down this small hole and twisted so that the cutting edge lies at the required angle to the bobbin, and is held firmly in place with the cutting point against the bobbin. The bobbin is then rotated and the point of the metal rod cuts a screw thread on the shank of the bobbin. This process can be stopped at any point just by pulling the cutter out of contact with the shank and removing the bobbin.

present day bobbin makers, but one only has to look at the beautifully pierced shanks of some of the antique bobbins to realise that some old craftsmen had this process down to a fine art. Take a close look at a mother and babe made by Archibald Abbott and you can clearly see, at either end of the slot, the curved cut produced by the circular cutter he used.

Bobbin makers of the last century, may not have enjoyed the range of tools, glues and materials which are available today, but they understood their tools, and knowing their limitations, used them to produce bobbins which are in no way inferior to those produced today.

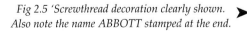

The workshop of the bobbin maker

two hundred years ago

would have been a very different sight

from that used by the bobbin maker today.

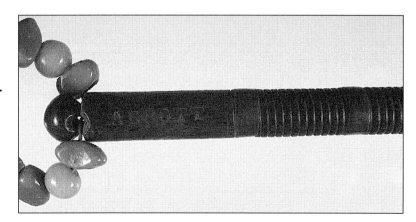

Fig 2.5 'Screwthread decoration clearly shown. ►
Also note the name ABBOTT stamped at the end.

Election bobbins

"Bedford Town Election"

Artist unknown. Dated 1835 but thought to depict the 1832 Election. Reproduced by kind permission of "Bedford Borough Council".

In the election campaigns before the Parliamentary Reform Bill of 1832, corruption was particularly widespread. Voting was by a show of hands, rather than secret ballot, and this system was easily abused. Candidates spent fortunes in their efforts to secure votes. In the Northampton Borough Election of 1818 one of the successful candidates was said to have spent £5,000, and the sponsors of the other successful candidate were said to have spent even more. Members of Parliament received no salary at this time, and many expected to recoup any expenses incurred during the campaign by using their influence for their own ends. The rewards could be great and this was often reflected in bitter and violent campaigns where the end seemed to justify the use of any means.

Inducements of all kinds were offered in an attempt to woo the voters, and one "free gift" which became quite popular in the lacemaking constituencies of Bedford, Buckingham and Northampton was a bobbin inscribed with the candidate's name and appropriate slogan e.g. Vote for Osborne. The names of over a dozen prospective M.P.s are known to have been immortalised in this way.

Close examination of any distinctive features of these bobbins may make it possible to find other bobbins which have been made by the same maker, and because it is not too difficult to find out which election a candidate took part in, an approximate date for the bobbin can be established. In some cases it is possible to be more specific than others, for example Mr. C. Hill was an unsuccessful candidate in two elections, but it is more likely that the bobbin was made for the 1830 election than for the 1835 campaign because corruption was reduced after the 1832 Parliamentary Reform Bill. When the bobbin refers to a candidate who successfully contested a number of elections, it becomes very difficult to determine which election they might have been made for and it is only possible to say that the bobbin was made between the dates of that candidate's first and last election campaign.

In this way election bobbins can provide useful information which may help towards dating other bobbins. Unfortunately election bobbins seem to be far less numerous than the famed "hanging" bobbins, and we have only been able to use a few of these bobbins in this way. However it is worth including a brief note on each known election bobbin so that anyone possessing such a bobbin might be able to use it in the same way.

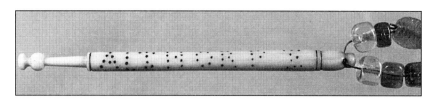

Fig. 3.1. "Vote For Althorpe", ➤
made by Jesse Compton.
(Courtesy of Northampton Museum
and Art Gallery.)

Northamptonshire Election Bobbins

"Vote For Althorpe", "Althorpe For Ever", "Althorpe And Milton" and "Milton For Ever".

John Charles Spencer, Viscount Althorp, was a member of the aristocracy living at Althorp Park, just outside Northampton. He had a long Parliamentary career representing Northampton from 1806-32. There is a bone bobbin inscribed "Vote For Althorpe" in the Abington Museum, Northampton, which we have been able to identify as the work of Jesse Compton. His bobbin making career began in the 1820s so this election bobbin was probably commissioned for one of the later elections contested by Viscount Althorp.

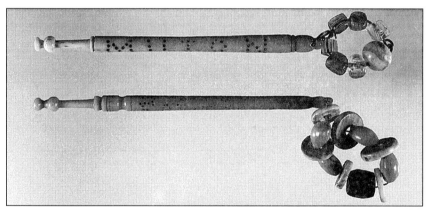

▲ Fig. 3.2. "Lord Milton", above, by Jesse Compton and "Lord John", below, possibly referring to Lord John Spencer Viscount Althorpe.

Viscount Althorp and Viscount Milton (the right Honourable Charles William Wentworth Fitzwilliam) stood together for Parliament in the year 1831. The bone bobbin commemorating this event could only have been made at that time. It is well made having two red bands above and below the horizontal inscription. The lettering is also red. Unfortunately we are unable to identify the maker of this bobbin. Another bobbin bearing the inscription "Althorpe and Milton" can be seen in the Bedford Museum and that particular bobbin was made by Jesse Compton.

It is most likely that the bobbin bearing the inscription "Milton for Ever" would have been made for the 1831 election when he stood with Viscount Althorp.

Northampton Borough

Northampton Borough was one of the dozen or so "householder" or "pot-walloper" boroughs which, before the 1832 Reform Bill, had the widest franchise in England. This gave all male householders resident in the Borough the right to vote providing they were not receiving alms or poor relief. This meant that approximately 60% of the adult males in Northampton were eligible to vote, so nearly every lacemaker's husband would be involved. This would explain why so many of the candidates contesting this seat gave away election bobbins.

It is an interesting footnote that voting was by show of hands (and it was not unknown for one man to put up both hands for one candidate) and if the issue was in doubt, as it always seemed to be, then during the following three or four days all those eligible to vote came and cast their votes which were then recorded alongside their name in a Poll Book.

Northampton Borough had two seats in the Commons, and a voter was allowed to split his two votes between two candidates, or he could cast just one vote for one candidate which of course made that single vote more valuable. Because the Poll Books were published and were made readily available after the election, it was only too easy for anyone to discover how an individual had voted and he might find himself discriminated against because of his political allegiance. This encouraged many electors to give one vote to each of the two most influential political factions of the time.

Because of the very liberal nature of its franchise, the Reform Bill did not help the voters of the Borough and in fact the number of those eligible to vote steadily decreased after the bill became law in 1832.

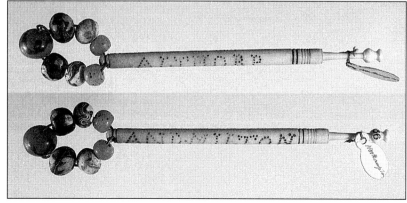

▲ Fig. 3.3 & 3.4. "Althorpe And Milton", maker unknown.
(Courtesy Bedford Borough Council.)

"Robinson For Ever"

Sir George Robinson, a member of the local gentry from Cranford, followed in the footsteps of his father who was MP for Northampton Borough from 1774 to 1780. His son had a much longer career, sitting for the same constituency from 1820 until 1832. He had unsuccessfully contested the 1818 election, when the rather more unscrupulous sponsors of another candidate circulated slanderous rumours about him. He seems to have been able to emerge relatively unscathed to not only be elected, but to gain more votes than any of the other candidates in the following four elections. He was a Whig who later supported the Reform Bill and he seems to have been able to avoid much of the corruption of the time and was one of the more respected Members of Parliament. This particular inscribed bobbin was made by Joseph Haskins of Bedford.

"Sir Ed Kerrison"

Sir Edward Kerrison represented Northampton in Parliament from 1818 until 1824 when he sat for Eye, retiring from Parliament in 1852. Whilst he was serving in parliament he was also serving in the army. He was at Waterloo, served in Spain, France and Holland. In 1851 whilst still an MP he became a General and later a Colonel of the 14th Light Dragoons. Even then they felt that being an MP was only part-time work !

The bobbin which we have seen bearing the inscription "Sir Ed Kerrison" precisely matches the style of "Robinson for Ever". It is unusual in its layout with individual letters set in bands around the bobbin. Joseph Haskins, as far as we know, was the only bobbinmaker who inscribed his election bobbins in this manner.

"Maberly for Ever"

Lt Colonel William Leader Maberly (1798-1885) was a member of the Maberly family who had made their fortune as service contractors supplying the army with boots and shoes during the Napoleonic Wars. At the age of seventeen he entered the army as a lieutenant colonel, but embarked upon a political career as soon as he was able. He was not old enough to contest the 1818 election, so his father sponsored Kerrison who was duly elected. To achieve this the Maberlys were said to have spent even more than the £5,000 it cost the other successful candidate to secure his seat. Maberly was one of the elected MPs for the Borough from 1820 - 30, before going on to sit for Shaftesbury and Chatham. He was first elected as a Tory, but during the ten

years he represented Northampton Borough, he transferred his allegiance to the Whigs. He became joint secretary of the General Post Office in 1836 and held that position for the next twenty years during which time he opposed all Roland Hill's schemes for reform. He was ruthless, unscrupulous and did not hesitate to use his position for his own gain.

"Gunning For Reform"

Sir Robert Henry Gunning contested the three elections of 1826, 1830 and 1831. He was successful in 1830, but his career in Parliament was of short duration as he was defeated at the next election by Robinson and Smith, who were declared reformers. It is most likely that the bobbin was commissioned for this last election when reform was the burning issue, but despite the sentiments expressed on the bobbin Gunning was not successful in his efforts to sway the voters.

"Smith For Ever"

It is most likely that the "Smith" referred to on this inscribed election bobbin is the Right Honourable Robert Vernon Smith. He was a Liberal and was elected to represent Northampton in 1831. This he did until June 1859 when he was created Lord Lyveden.

Unfortunately on the bobbins inscribed "Smith For Ever" no initial is ever marked so it is possible that the Smith referred to might be John Smith, a Whig, who was elected for Buckinghamshire in 1831 and retired in 1835. The bobbin might also refer to Abel Smith, a Whig, who represented Buckinghamshire 1812-1818, 1830-32. There was also a George Smith who represented Wendover, Buckinghamshire between 1806 and 1830. Finally the Right Honourable John Smith, a Whig, must be considered. He represented Wendover, Buckinghamshire between 1818 and 1820, and also sat for Buckinghamshire between the years 1820 to 1830. So take your pick !

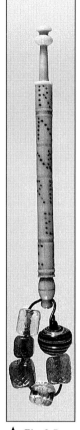

▲ Fig. 3.5 "Robinson For Ever", made by Joseph Haskins.

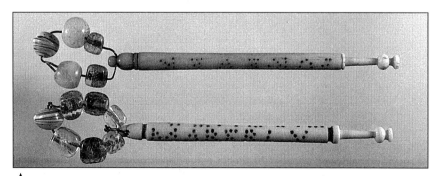

▲ Fig. 3.6 "Smith For Ever", "Maberly For Ever", both made by Jesse Compton. If the head is held in the right hand and the bobbin rotated the names Smith & Maberly can be clearly read but the words "For Ever" are upside down.

Fig. 3.8. "Tavistock For Ever" and a fairing
both made by the same unknown maker. ➤

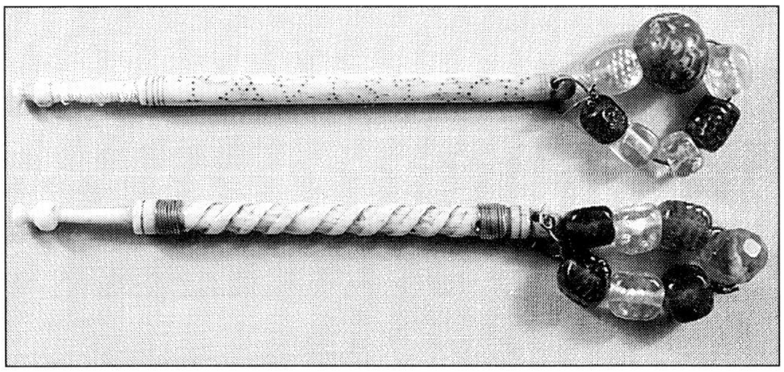

Buckinghamshire Election Bobbins

"Chandos For Ever"

Richard Plantagenet Nugent Grenville Chandos Temple, Marquis of Chandos was the heir of the Duke of Buckingham. He sat for Buckingham from 1818-39 and it would have been very appropriate in this lace-making area to distribute election bobbins to gain votes. Unlike Bedford and Northampton, Buckingham had a very narrow franchise and it was probably largely due to the influence and patronage of his father that he secured his place in Parliament.

"Tavistock For Ever"

Lord George William Russell, Marquis of Tavistock, was the eldest son of the Duke of Bedford. He was an MP for many years, representing first Peterborough and then Bedford Borough from 1812-30. It would perhaps have been towards the end of this period that he might have commissioned such bobbins.

Bedford Museum has three election bobbins inscribed for Whitbread, Polhill and Crawley. These three candidates contested the 1832 and 1835 elections for the Borough, and it therefore seems quite likely, that it was for one of these campaigns, most probably the earlier of the two that these bobbins would have been commissioned and distributed.

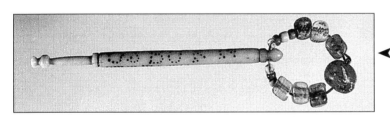

◀ Fig. 3.7. "Vote For Osborn", maker unknown.
(Courtesy of Bedford Borough Council.)

Bedfordshire Election Bobbins

"Vote For Osborne" & "Osborne For Ever"

John Osborne was the elected member for Bedfordshire in the years 1806-1807 and 1818-20, so this would tend to indicate that distributing election bobbins probably began at an earlier date in Bedfordshire than it did in Northampton.

"Whitbread"

Samuel Whitbread sat for Bedford from 1768 until his son took over his seat in 1790. Samuel Whitbread Junior, held this seat until his suicide in 1815, and then his son William Henry Whitbread, represented Bedford from 1818 until 1835. He also unsuccessfully contested the 1835 and 1841 elections. Although it is impossible to be certain, the bobbin inscribed " Whitbread" was probably commissioned by William, as it was during the years in which he stood for Parliament that election bobbins seem to have been most popular.

Bedford Borough

Like Northampton, Bedford had an extremely wide franchise. All freemen and householders resident in the borough were eligible to vote. This no doubt included the husbands of many lace-makers, so, as in Northampton, distributing free bobbins, with suitable slogans, would have been a popular way of gaining publicity.

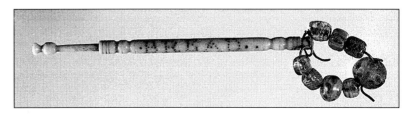

▲ Fig. 3.9. "Whit-bread", maker unknown.
(Courtesy of Bedford Borough Council.)

"Polhill For Ever"

Frederick Polhill was a captain in the King's dragoon guards, and for some time leased the Drury Lane Theatre. He was returned as one of the two MPs for Bedford Borough from 1830-32 and from 1835-47, when he was defeated. He took an active part in many of the issues put before the parliament of the day, and seems to have had the best interests of his electors at heart.

Fig. 3.10. "Polhill For Ever".
▼ *(Courtesy of Bedford Borough Council.)*

"Crawley For Ever"

Samuel Crawley was the elected MP for Honiton from 1818–26. At this time Honiton was another "potwalloper" Borough with a very wide franchise. It was also one of the most venal boroughs in the country. Crawley was MP for Bedford from 1832–41. We have not been able to discover whether Crawley had any particular links with the lacemaking industry, but it is probably just coincidence that he should represent one noted lacemaking centre, before moving to another.

The election bobbin which has been repaired with a spliced top is most interesting for the inscription reads "Crawley For Ever 1833". This is the only election bobbin which we have seen which has been dated. The repair itself is worth noting for it is so well executed. The two parts fit precisely and they are held together with two pewter rivets.

Inducements of all kinds

were offered in an attempt

to woo the voters

It is interesting to note that in the 1832 election contested by Crawley, Whitbread and Polhill, Capt Polhill was defeated by Crawley by three votes. Capt Polhill petitioned against this result, accusing Crawley of bribery and sharp practice because many people entered on the register of voters, were in fact, not eligible to vote. Although 42 names were struck off the list of voters, Crawley retained his seat.

Finding himself defeated at the 1837 election, Crawley accused Henry Stuart, Esq, of similar malpractices and as a result of this successful petition, Crawley was returned for Bedford Borough in Stuart's place.

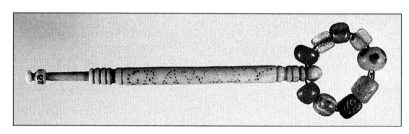

▲ *Fig. 3.11. "Crawley For Ever."*
(Courtesy of Bedford Borough Council.)

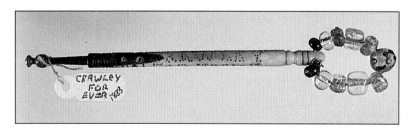

◀ *Fig. 3.12. "Crawley For Ever 1833".*
An unusual spliced repair.

Fig. 3.13. A most unusual election bobbin made ▶
by Jesse Compton. "Suckess To The Pillow Lace".
(Courtesy of
Northampton Museum and Art Gallery.)

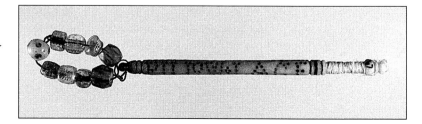

"Hanging Bobbins"

There were six executions in the nineteenth century which were commemorated on inscribed bobbins. These bobbins, like election bobbins, can be useful in helping to establish the years in which a bobbin maker was producing bobbins.

"Matthias And William Lilley 1829"

Bobbins with this inscription were made to commemorate the execution of two brothers who were hanged at Biddenham for the attempted murder of a gamekeeper who had caught them poaching. There was some doubt about whether the gun they carried went off accidentally, or whether it was a serious attempt to kill the gamekeeper, but they were found guilty of attempted murder, which was a capital offence at the time. It is thought that unlike the other five "hanging" bobbins these were made out of sympathy for the two unfortunate young men. In all the years which we have researched into the history of lace bobbins we have never yet seen an example of this hanging bobbin and we are unsure whether they exist.

"Sarah Dazeley Hung 1843"

Sarah was hanged at Bedford at the age of 22, for the murder of her second husband whom she poisoned with arsenic. There is a strong possibility that she was also responsible for the premature death of her first husband.

The following information was taken from a poster printed by J. S. & W. Merry Bedford in 1843.

The Execution Of Sarah Dazeley

who was executed on the new drop in front of the county gaol at Bedford, on Saturday 5th of August 1843 for the wilful murder of her husband, William Dazeley, at Wrestlingworth.

The prisoners maiden name was Reynolds, and was the daughter of Mr P. Reynolds of Potton, hair dresser. The first husband of this unhappy woman was named Simon Mead by whom she had a daughter, which when 9 months old died very suddenly. About five months after the death of Mead she was married to William Dazeley, her unfortunate victim, who was buried in Wrestlingworth churchyard, with the following remarkable verse on the tombstone.

> "The strong may think their house a rock
> Yet soon as Jesus calls
> Some sickness brings a fatal shock
> And down the building falls."

Since the condemnation of the unhappy woman she has been confined in the condemned cell, and attended by a female both night and day, with whom she has frequently conversed in a light and cheerful manner, appearing to think that the sentence would not be carried into execution, and that it was merely for the purpose of extorting a confession. On being visited on Wednesday by her friends in the presence of the chaplain, they wished her to make a full confession of her crime, when she is reported to have said, "I won't make a confession, I did not do it, he (meaning Dazeley) poisoned the child and afterwards poisoned himself".

At the hour of 4 o'clock this morning the workmen commenced preparing the drop for the execution and the people of the neighbouring villages began to arrive, amongst whom were a great many from Potton and Wrestlingworth, the scene of her crimes, and to whom she was well known. About 10 o'clock she attended chapel and the usual service was performed. On the arrival of the under Sheriff (with an escort of Javelin men) the body of the unfortunate woman was demanded and they then proceeded to the press room where the operation of pinioning her was performed. The procession, consisting of the under Sheriff, chaplain, Gaoler,

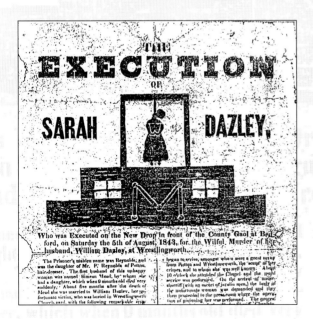

◀ *Fig. 4.1 A poster "advertising" the hanging.*

Turnkey and Javelin men, began to move, the chaplain reading the burial service, commencing with, " I am the resurrection and the life." On arrival at the place of execution she joined the chaplain in prayer and shook hands with the attendants, no extraordinary emotion or trepidation being perceptible in her manner, a slight sigh appeared to escape from her when the cap was drawn over her face and the rope adjusted. The executioner then retired leaving her standing alone on the drop, when the signal being given, the bolt was drawn and the unfortunate woman was launched into eternity. She was observed to struggle for a few seconds when life became extinct. The body after hanging the usual time was removed for burial within the precincts of the gaol, according to the sentence of the learned judge. May the Lord have mercy on her immortal soul, and may we be led to take care of our own – the aim and object of public execution."

"I won't make a confession,

I did not do it"

As yet we have not seen a Sarah Dazeley hanging bobbin and so it is impossible to be certain whether such bobbins exist.

"Joseph Castle Hung 1860"

Joseph Castle was hung on Saturday 31st March 1860 at Bedford gaol for the murder of his wife. J. S. & W. Merry again printed a poster to advertise and commemorate the event. Below are some details taken from that poster.

The Life, Trial, Confession, And Execution Of Joseph Castle

"This unhappy young man, who was only 24 years of age, was a native of Ware, in Hertfordshire. His parents were industrious and respectable persons, and their character unimpeachable for uprightness and integrity. His brother is now carrying on a respectable business in that place as a

▲ *Fig. 4.2. A wood cut taken from the Joseph Castle poster.*

baker. Joseph was always of a nervous temperament, and at times exceedingly irritable. In August 1857, he married Jane Whitcroft, of York Street, Luton, to whom he seemed strongly attached and dotingly fond. But his wayward disposition and irritable temper, before long, rendered them unhappy, and they frequently quarrelled. For the last five or six months previous to this melancholy affair, Joseph Castle and his wife lodged with his uncle, James Castle, at Ware. There also they had frequent quarrels, through his unfounded fits of jealousy. On one occasion he told her to leave him; but when she prepared to do so, he tore up her clothes to prevent her from going. They had no children. On the 8th of August, 1859, she determined to leave him, and went to the house of her parents, Thomas and Frances Whitcroft, in York Street Luton. When he found she had gone he followed her to her father's house, and unfortunately persuaded her to return with him, and on their way back he murdered her by cutting her throat and then stabbing her in the front of her neck, which completed the dreadful deed. He then threw the knife over the hedge, and dragged her body into a pit or dell by the side of the road."

The poster then continues to detail the trial, his conduct and confession. The next excerpt deals with his execution.

The Execution

"No execution having taken place here since that of Sarah Dazeley, about 16 years ago, the concourse of people

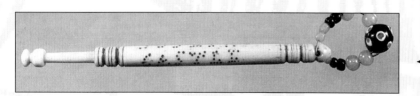

◄ *Fig. 4.3. A Joseph Castle hanging bobbin made by the "blunt end" man.*

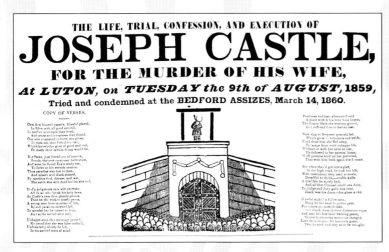

THE LIFE, TRIAL, CONFESSION, AND EXECUTION OF
JOSEPH CASTLE,
FOR THE MURDER OF HIS WIFE,
At LUTON, on TUESDAY the 9th of AUGUST, 1859,
Tried and condemned at the BEDFORD ASSIZES, March 14, 1860.

COPY OF VERSES.

Fig. 4.4.. Illustrated above part of the execution poster.

The flat roof of the building on which the drop was erected was unusually boarded in front and the ends, which obstructed the view and disappointed spectators.

At length, the fatal signal being given, the bolt was withdrawn, and he was launched into eternity, amidst the sobs and tears and melancholy exclamations of the assembled multitude. May the Lord have mercy on his immortal soul; and may we be led to take care of our own — the aim and object of public executions. — Reader farewell."

It is said that Jane Castle's family gave a party on the evening of the execution, and each guest was given a bobbin "Joseph Castle 1860. " Certainly many such souvenirs were sold that day and it is one of the "hanging" bobbins more commonly seen today.

assembled might be counted by thousands. It was immense. The windows of the houses were filled with pretty faces, and the tops of buildings and projections of all kinds of erections exhibited human beings in every direction.

May the Lord have mercy

on his immortal soul

This day (Saturday March 31st), at twelve at noon, the usual preparations and arrangements having been made in the prison, the mournful procession advanced up the steps to the drop in front of the gaol, over the entrance, the chaplain reading the burial service as they proceeded. All present seemed more deeply impressed with the awfulness of this melancholy scene than the victim himself to the violated laws of his country, who seemed determined to brave it out to his utmost, but at his last moments his lips appeared to move as if he were engaged in secret prayer.

"Franz Muller Hung 1864"

This is the only execution commemorated on a bobbin which did not take place in Bedford. It had created wide public interest as Muller was the first man to commit murder on a railway train, and was executed for his crime at Newgate prison in London.

The bobbin shown in the photograph was made by Bobbin Brown of Cranfield.

Fig. 4.5, 4.6 & 4.7. Three sides of the Franz Muller hanging bobbin. ➤

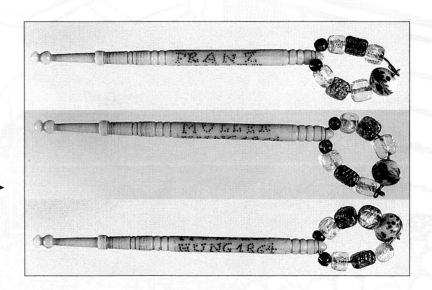

"William Worsley Hung 1868"

William Worsley and Levi Welch murdered a man at Luton, but Welch turned King's evidence and accused Worsley of striking the critical blow, and thus escaped the gallows. Worsley was the last man to be publicly hanged at Bedford and inscribed bobbins were extremely popular souvenirs, making these one of the most common of the six hanging bobbins.

▼ *Fig. 4.8 & 4.9. Two William Worsley hanging bobbins, both made by "Bobbin" Brown.*

"William Bull Hung 1871"

William Bull murdered Sarah Marshall, a harmless old woman who was probably half witted. He was very drunk at the time and killed the poor lady in a particularly brutal manner, so there was great public satisfaction when Bull was brought to justice, and even though the hanging was not public, many people bought inscribed bobbins to commemorate the event.

It must be understood that public executions acted as a warning to the population. If you committed a crime then you would be dealt with severely. Justice had to be seen to be done and therefore the day of the hanging was declared a public holiday to encourage all to come and see the execution take place. In and around the area of the prison there would be market stalls and even a fair. Needless to say local bobbin makers were not slow to take advantage of such a gathering of lacemakers, they would also have attended the hanging to sell their wares which would, no doubt, have included inscribed bobbins to commemorate the event.

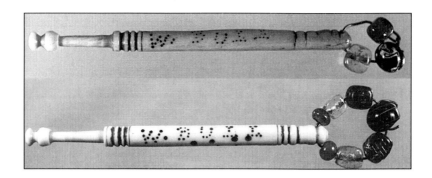

▲ *Fig. 4.10, 4.11. The two "Bull" hanging bobbins above were made by the "blunt end" man.*
The rather poorly lettered "Bull" hanging bobbin
▼ *beneath (Fig. 4.12) was made by Arthur Wright of Cranfield.*

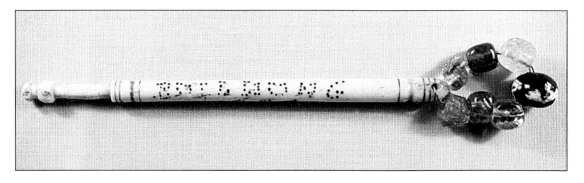

Trade Bobbins

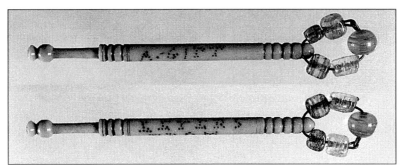

◀ Fig. 5.1 & 5.2. Two sides of the same bobbin. "A Gift From Leters" (misspelt), made by the "blunt end" man.

B obbins inscribed "A Gift From Lester" have become well known and much sought after because of there link with the lace business owned by the Lester family in Bedford, but there were other lesser known lace dealers who also commissioned inscribed bobbins.

"A Gift From Lester"

According to Thomas Wright in his book "The Romance of The Lace Pillow", Mr Thomas Lester was a terrible autocrat casting fear amongst the lacemakers who came to Bedford to sell him their lace. The lacemaker, if her work was shoddy, might well have her fingers trapped in a drawer as a punishment, but if her work was well done then she might be rewarded with the present of a bobbin inscribed "A Gift From Lester". These bobbins would also have served to advertise Lester's business amongst the lacemakers and might have encouraged the better workers to take their lace to the Lester's shop in Bedford.

The bobbin in the photograph is inscribed "A Gift From Leters", others we have seen are correctly spelt "A Gift From Lesters" or even just "From Lesters". This particular bobbin was made by the turner we know only as the "blunt end man". He was a rather poor worker and it is perhaps surprising that the Lesters commissioned him to make their bobbins. We have seen a number of bobbins inscribed for Lester made by Bobbin Brown of Cranfield, which is far more understandable, as Brown's work was of a considerably higher standard.

▼ Fig. 5.3 "Cut off day". A lacemaker prepares to sell her work to a lace dealer.

"Cut-Off Day"

The great event to the Lace Maker is "Cut-off" Day, when she unwinds the dainty Lace upon which she has spent so many hours of labour, and measures it up ready for the Lace Buyer.

Fig. 5.4. "Reckles", see next page. ➤

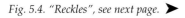
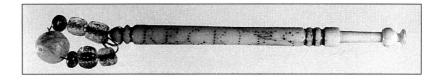

"Reckles"

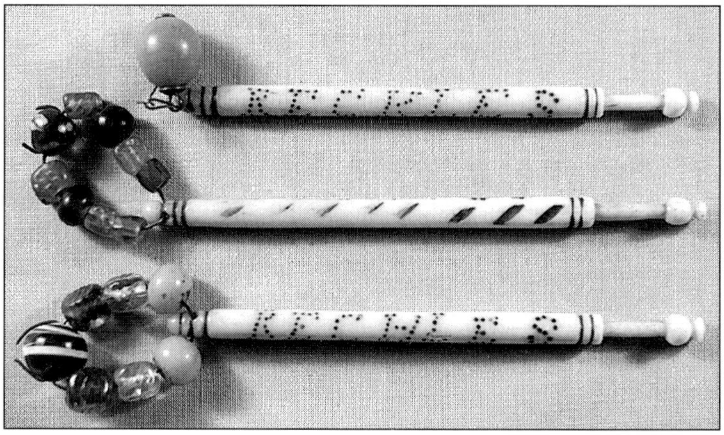

When we discovered one bobbin inscribed "Reckles" we accepted it as a person's name, but when we came upon three identical bobbins from three different sources we began to wonder about the significance of the inscription. In an 1832 directory Joseph Reckles was listed as a lace dealer in Goose Pasture Lane (now Meadow Lane), Kettering, Northants. Perhaps he used these inscribed bobbins as gifts to help advertise his lace business. Unfortunately we cannot identify the maker of these bobbins at present.

▲ Fig. 5.5. Three more "Reckles" bobbins. Maker unknown.

"Emma Malt"

Pauline Robinson, a present day lacemaker, having spoken about lacemaking on the BBC Radio "Woman's Hour" in 1970, was sent some antique bobbins by Phyllis Ingram an elderly lacemaker. Amongst the bobbins were a dozen or more identical bone bobbins inscribed E. Malt. On enquiring about these bobbins Ms Ingram related that they were given to her by Emma Malt in 1907. Emma Malt was by then a very old woman who had a small drapers shop in Thrapston, Northamptonshire. Her great pride was that she was the illegitimate daughter of the Duke of Wellington and a gamekeeper's daughter at

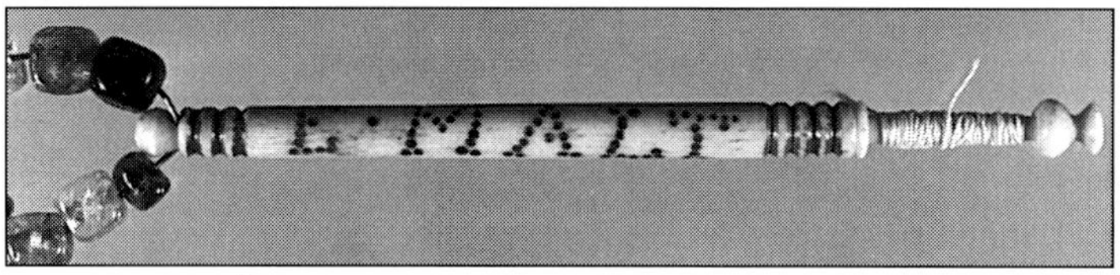

▲ Fig. 5.6. "Emma Malt" bobbin made by Archibald Abbott.

Woodford House. The Duke, she tells, used to stay at Woodford where he had a tower built giving a view of what he, the Duke, said was exactly like the field of Waterloo. Ms Ingram also stated that Emma Malt was very like the Duke's picture, had great dignity and was proud of her ducal blood.

With so many bobbins inscribed E. Malt, (made by Archibald Abbott of Bedford), linked to the fact that Emma ran a drapers shop, it would seem likely that these bobbins were originally intended to be used as advertising or trade bobbins.

"Queen Caroline"

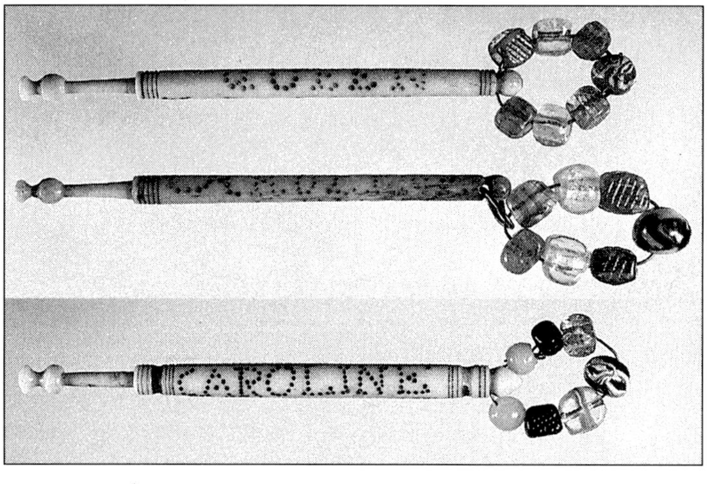

At the beginning of the 19th century we had a Prince of Wales with a wife he did not love and who did not love him. She eventually left England to live in Italy.

In 1820 George, Prince of Wales, became King George IV of England. When his wife Caroline realised that she would be Queen she hurried back from Italy. The Prime Minister, at the King's request, tried through a Parliamentary Bill to deprive her of her rank and attempted to dissolve the marriage. After a long trial the Bill was abandoned, to the great joy of the population of Great Britain.

▲ Fig. 6.1. Top inscription "Queen For Ever".
Middle inscription "Queen Caroline".
Lower inscription "Caroline For Ever". Makers unknown.

In the 1820's a number of bobbins were made with the inscription "Queen Caroline" or "Queen for Ever" to commemorate the event and show support for the Queen.

Although we are not able to identify the maker of these bobbins they may help to date similar bobbins in other collections.

Of course there are many other "Royal" inscriptions such as "Queen Victoria", "Prince Albert", "Queen Adelaide" (this particular bobbin can be seen in Bedford Museum), but do not be confused by "King David", "King Pharaoh", or "King Solomon" as these are religious inscriptions.

Religious Inscriptions

The view of 19th century village life can be confusing, for on the one hand the villagers appear to be God-fearing people, attending church on Sunday, being well acquainted with the Bible, even having bobbins on their lace pillows with religious inscriptions, but when the censuses and records are studied, illegitimate births, minor law breaking, drunkenness and a general "earthy" quality gives quite a different picture.

Many inscriptions are quite simple, "God Is Love", "The Lord Will Provide", "I Love Jesus", others are more specific. One particular bobbin made by Jesse Compton reads "Joseph Best P.M. Minister 1844", it was not until the owner spent some time researching this name that it was discovered that the two initials stood for Primitive Minister. Joseph Best was a Methodist Minister who spent some time in Buckingham, he must have made quite an impression upon at least one lacemaker for his name to be recorded upon a bone bobbin. It is known that there are two bobbins (so far discovered) with this inscription. Finally a most ominous religious inscription on a bobbin made by "Bobbin" Brown..........."Prepair To Meet Thy God".

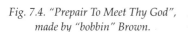

Fig. 7.1. "The Lord Will Provide".
*Maker unknown. A sad comment from a time when
no one else would provide if one were old or infirm.*

Some religious inscriptions found on bobbins have other purposes. For example, if a lacemaker accepted, a full set of inscribed bobbins making up the whole of The Lord's Prayer, from her young man, then it was considered as binding as an engagement ring. As we have seen so few inscribed with any part of The Lord's Prayer, it does not appear to have been a very popular option.

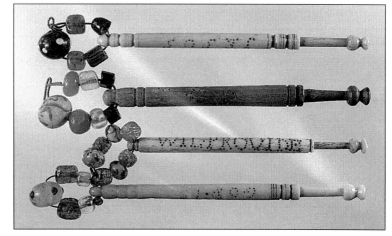

▼ Fig. 7.3. "Joseph Best PM Minister 1844",
made by Jesse Compton.

▲ Fig. 7.2. From the top down. "I Love Jesus",
made by the "blunt end" man. (Upside down).
*"Jesus", a loose spiral wood inscription
made by James Compton.*
"The Lord Wil Provide", maker unknown.
*"God Is Love",
made by the "blunt end" man. (Upside down)*

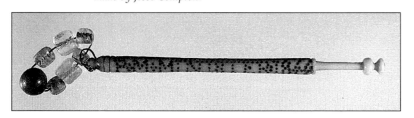

Fig. 7.4. "Prepair To Meet Thy God", ▶
made by "bobbin" Brown.

"Music Hall" Inscriptions

The music hall must have been a most influential, exciting and exotic form of entertainment for young lacemakers used only to the hardship of rural village life. So perhaps it is surprising that this form of inscription is not more common. After a special evening's entertainment amongst friends, how pleasant to record the event upon a bobbin, so that when back at work in the cottage, the memory of that evening might be rekindled by the turn of a bobbin.

▲ Fig. 8.1. "Slap Bang Here We Go Again", made by "bobbin" Brown.

The following three inscriptions are a few of those inspired by popular Music Hall songs.

"Wait For The Wagon". This was made by the "blunt end" man. We have seen another of his bobbins with a similar inscription but the word "wait" was misspelt "wate".

"Poop Goes The Wesal". No doubt this was meant to read "Pop Goes The Weasel." Maker unknown.

"Slap Bang Here We Go Again". We are informed that this line comes from the Jolly Dog Polka. This particular bobbin, shown in the photograph, was made by "Bobbin Brown."

▲ Fig. 8.3

▼ Fig. 8.2. "Poop Goes The Wesal" and "Wait For The Wagon" both made by the "blunt end" man.

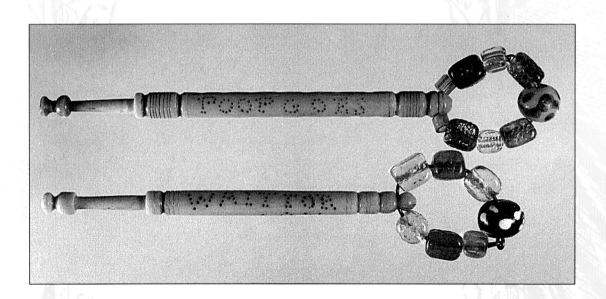

The "Bitted" Man. C 1810-1830

Fig. 9.1 & 9.2. A typical head and tail from a bobbin made by the "bitted" man.

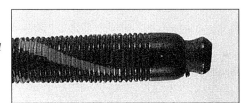

The "Bitted" man

I t is unfortunate that we cannot identify this bobbin maker for he was an exceptionally gifted worker, but we do know that he was definitely making bobbins around 1810–1820. Clearly he specialised in producing bitted bobbins, developing his skills in making this style of bobbin to the very highest level, working in both wood and bone. We hope you will forgive us for using the name "Bitted" man but it is more personal than identifying him using just a letter, Maker C., as we did in our first book.

As bobbin makers ourselves, we appreciate just how difficult it is to construct a satisfactory design for a bitted bobbin, as all the grooves must be made and filled with slivers of Boxwood whilst the bobbin is still a blank which is square in section. This blank is then shaped in the lathe in the same way as any other bobbin. The skill lies in being able to visualise how the change in section, from square blank to round bobbin, will affect the inserted "bits" and manipulating the angles and shapes of the initial grooves accordingly.

Many of the simple designs merely require diagonal cuts to be made on opposite sides of the blank, but some more elaborately inlaid bobbins were achieved by cutting into all four sides. Others which have crossing lines or curves, must have a series of cuts made in one direction which are filled and trimmed before a second series of cuts in the opposite direction is made and similarly treated. These must be done with great accuracy as the slightest deviation is greatly magnified when the blank is turned, and the finished effect is easily spoiled. Long, curved lines seem to be unique to this bobbin maker, perhaps because they require a specially made cutting tool similar to a tre-panning saw, to which other makers might not have had access.

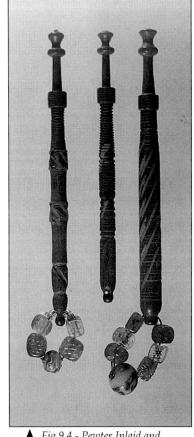

Apart from the breath-taking complexity of design, his bobbins bear several other important distinctive features. The most useful, from the point of identification, is the rather longer than average collar at the top of the shank, which, like the rest of the shank, is covered with closely spaced incised lines. Below this collar, the shank regains its even cylindrical shape rather sharply, forming very marked shoulders at this point.

Both the head and tail of the bobbins supply further characteristic pointers with which to identify this craftsman's work. The head in particular, is of unusual shape and

▲ *Fig 9.4 - Pewter Inlaid and Bitted Bobbins*

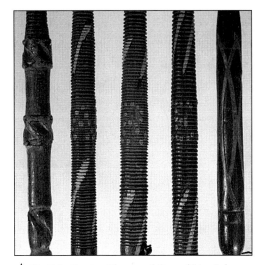

▲ *Fig 9.5 - Pewter, Thorn and Curved Line Inlay*

▲ *Fig 9.3 - Bees Knees, plain, two coloured and wood leopard*

▲ Fig 9.6
An unusual Beaded Shank Decorated Bobbin

proportions looking very much like an apple core. The bulb is rather squashed in appearance, above which the short neck flares gently upwards towards the rim, this section may comprise more than half the height of the whole head. This is not usually the case, as the heads of most bobbins have as much if not more length taken up by the bulb.

The end of the shank curves in neatly to a tail of smaller diameter which is drilled to take the wire of the spangle.

Beside these fine examples of bitted bobbins this maker also produced other remarkable work such as thorn inlay. To produce this type of decoration, fine holes are drilled to form the chosen initials then small thorns, probably from Hawthorn or Blackthorn, are glued and gently hammered into the holes. The thorn is then trimmed close to the bobbin surface leaving a pale dot against the darker wood of the bobbin body.

Occasionally a wooden or bone bobbin might have a small area inlaid with pewter. The design of this inlay usually follows the same form, close to the top and bottom of the bobbin where two bands are set a short distance apart. These are joined by spiral grooves giving a twisted effect. Unfortunately the pewter of many of his bobbins has deteriorated badly over the years.

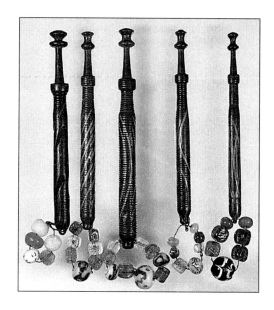

▲ *Fig 9.7 - Curved Line "Bitted" Bobbins*

We have been able to date this maker's work from the inscribed bobbins he has produced. These bobbins with the exception of the thorn inlay are worked in bone and they follow a similar form to his other bobbins. There is a large collar at the top of the bobbin and the rest of the shank is covered with closely spaced incised lines. Over these lines the drill dotted inscription is formed often accompanied by crosses, feather patterns or hatched lines. More often the inscription is just a set of initials or names and date, general inscriptions are much less common.

The elongated collar, the shaping of the shank, the unobtrusive tail, the unusual proportions of the head and the closely spaced incised lines covering the shank and collar, are all characteristic features of this maker's work.

He was a craftsman of rare creative flair, a great technician, whose use of curved and crossed lines must arouse any modern bobbin maker's deep admiration.

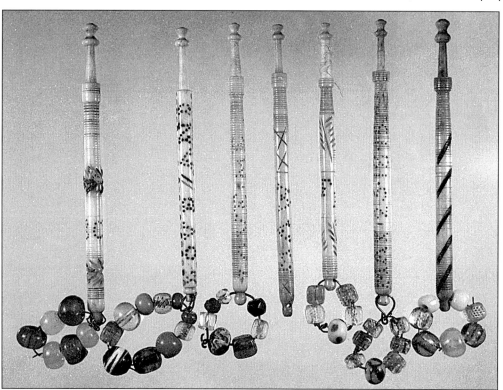

◄ *Fig. 9.8. A selection of bone inscribed and bitted bobbins.*

Jesse and James Compton

Thomas Wright in his book "Romance Of The Lace Pillow", states that "there were two famous bobbin makers at Deanshanger, Jesse Compton and his son James". According to the same writer, James made a wooden bobbin from the famous Wakes Oak of Whittlebury forest, which was burnt down by schoolboys in 1866. Wright says that this bobbin, inscribed "Wakes Oak", belonged to the Reverend A. J. Roberts who gathered together an enviable collection of lace bobbins during his lifetime. His daughter gave this collection, including the Wakes Oak bobbin, to Northampton Museum in 1950. Also in this collection is a very important bone bobbin with the spiral inscription "A New Years Gift For 1884 By J. Compton". J. Compton must refer to James, as his father Jesse, died in 1856. The lettering is coloured red and blue just as Thomas Wright says James used. It is very likely that the description of how the dots were coloured, which the Reverend Roberts gave to Thomas Wright, refers to the methods he saw James Compton using, as the Reverend Roberts also lived in the Parish of Passenham (of which Deanshanger is a part) and his cousin Frances, married James Compton's youngest surviving son in 1876.

So we were able to see two bobbins, one in wood and one in bone, which were definitely made by James Compton. However, it was not until we visited Aylesbury Museum, that we were able to identify the work of his father Jesse. Here we found two bone bobbins with precisely the same spiral inscription "Sarah Luckett Died November 10th Aged 56". One was indisputably the work of James Compton, bearing all the familiar characteristics, but the other had a tail end and head of quite a different, and up until that point, un-named maker. The similarities between the two were quite unmistakable, both had a double line at the top of the shank and a single line at the bottom, both used the same style of lettering, but more convincing than any other feature was the way in which both makers wrote the figure five in the inscription, no other bobbin maker left the top line off this figure in this manner.

This led us to look more closely at other inscribed bobbins which we had attributed to this un-named maker and to compare them with some of James's work. The similarities between the two became even more evident. We had already

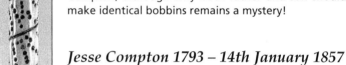

Fig. 10.1
Note the top
figure 5.

noted a large number of inscriptions, particularly spiral inscriptions, which had been made by this maker and the date span of these inscriptions indicated that he started his bobbin making career in the 1820's but the vast bulk of his dated bobbins fell in the 1830's and 40's. This is entirely consistent with the theory that the maker was James's father, Jesse Compton.

It is perfectly natural that a father, teaching his son how to make bobbins, should teach him to produce bobbins which were very similar to his own. James later did develop one or two features which enable us to tell his work from that of his father's, but his earlier bobbins are extremely closely modelled on those of his father, and it is sometimes very difficult to tell their bobbins apart. We therefore feel confident in stating that the second Sarah Luckett bobbin was the work of Jesse Compton, although why both father and son should make identical bobbins remains a mystery!

Jesse Compton 1793 – 14th January 1857

Jesse Compton was the son of James and Mary Compton. He was born in 1793 in Uphaven, Wiltshire, where his father was a farmer. In 1817, the now 24 year old, Jesse made his way to Lincolnshire. In the Lincolnshire archives, there are records of the "Thomas A'Becket" sessions at Kirton dated Friday 18th July 1817. These archives reveal that as punishment for vagrancy, Jesse Compton was to be detained for 13 days in the Kirton House of Correction, then publicly whipped, and sent back to Uphaven. This was the harshest sentence handed out at that session. The removal order required that the offender be escorted to each county boundary there to be transferred into the custody of the next official so ensuring his return to Wiltshire. For some reason Jesse only reached Hanslope in Buckinghamshire where he must have found work. Here he met and married Catherine. His rehabilitation was complete for we have discovered no other records of wrong doing.

It is not until the baptism of his fifth child in 1838 that Jesse describes himself as a bobbin maker. He also described himself as a turner on his eldest son's marriage lines in 1845. These are the only two occasions when he does not describe himself as a Hawker or labourer, '

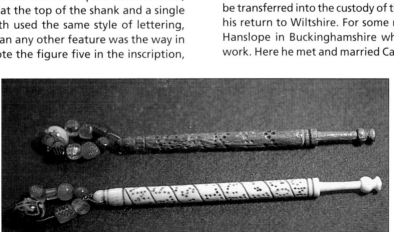

Fig. 10.2. "Wakes oak", and "A New Years Gift For 1884 By J. Compton."
(Courtesy of Northampton Museum and Art Gallery.)

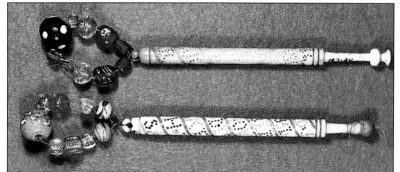

◄ *Fig. 10.3. Upper bobbin made by Jesse Compton, the lower bobbin made by James Compton. The inscription on both reads, "Sarah Luckett Died November 10th 1851 Aged 56." (Photograph by Courtesy of Buckinghamshire County Museum.)*

which is perhaps a little surprising when he produced such a quantity of bobbins in the 1830's and 40's.

Thomas Wright, referring to Jesse's inscribed bobbins, states that they were generally coloured with green and chrome yellow, but we have found no evidence to support this, most of the inscriptions which do retain any trace of their original colouring are red and green.

Because he was producing bobbins at a time when lace-making was going through a relatively prosperous period, his bobbins were surely well-used and many are now markedly thinner in the centre section of the shank. This makes some of the inscriptions very hard to read as the dots have almost completely worn away. The bone he used has also taken on a rather yellowed, translucent quality, as opposed to the dense whiteness of so many of the bobbins made by his son.

▲ *Fig. 10.4. A typical head and tail produced by Jesse Compton.*

The majority of his bobbins were very much slimmer than those of his son. This may be due to the fact that at the time when he was making bobbins, the lace being produced was of a very much finer quality. Because the thread used was so much finer and so many bobbins were needed to make even a narrow piece of lace, slimmer bobbins would have been much more suitable than the thicker, heavier bobbins which his son made twenty and thirty years later.

The head of his bobbins was made up of a rather compressed bulb shape and a very thin short neck which flared sharply up towards the top rim. Because the short neck was so narrow and the bobbins so well used, the thread

soon began to cut a groove at this point and the top section became very vulnerable and many of Jesse's bobbins which survive today, have lost this top part completely.

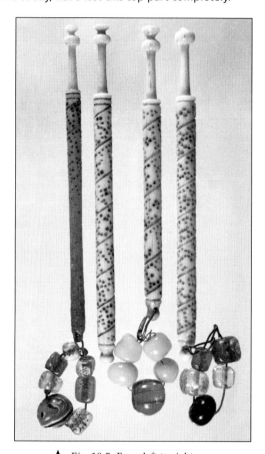

▲ *Fig. 10.5. From left to right.*
"A Present From J. S. 1838."
Note the worn centre section, typical of many of Jesse's bobbins.
"James Compton Mary Ann Compton 1841." (No spangle.)
"Respect The Giver J. S. 1836."
"S. Hipperson P. Methodist Preacher 1845."
(Does P stand for primitive?). Note the missing section of the head.

The end of his shank curved neatly into a small "knob" which was drilled to take the spangle. It is this shaping of the tail end which gives an important clue when distinguishing between Jesse's bobbins, and those of his son.

Many of Jesse's inscribed bone bobbins are written horizontally along the length of the shank, but by far the larg-

◀ *Fig. 10.6.*
Head and tail shape
of Jesse's pewter
inlaid bobbins.

of unknown material (probably antimony which helped to improve the lustre of the pewter) and only 2% consisted of lead. Tin is very easily affected by corrosive agents, and the constant handling of the bobbin during lacemaking allowed the perspiration passed from the lacemaker's fingers to build up and attack the tin in the pewter, causing the inlay to deteriorate. When pewter mugs and plates were in daily use, they would have been frequently washed, thus eliminating such an accumulation of corrosive elements.

Once the surface of the pewter inlay on the bobbin began to corrode the bobbin became rough and uncomfortable to handle and it would perhaps have been discarded by the lacemaker. Alternately she may have attempted to make it smoother to the touch by removing the affected pewter — much of which had become so weak that it had probably already started to crumble away. This would account for so many of his bobbins having empty grooves where the pewter work should be.

est proportion are inscribed in a spiral fashion. The lettering he used was sharp and neat and was often embellished with serifs, his figure one and his letter I being identical. His spelling was not perfect as can be seen from such inscriptions as "Suckess to the Pillow Lace" and "My Hart is Fixt I Cannot Range". During the first part of the nineteenth century there was a good sale for bobbins and judging by the number of general inscriptions which Jesse made e.g. "I Wish To Wed The Lad I Love", he probably carried a stock of such mottoes as well as taking orders for more personal inscriptions.

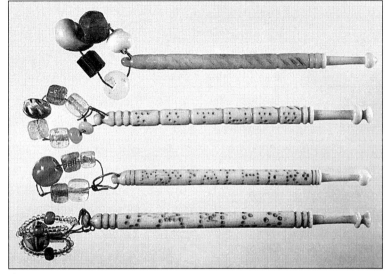

▲ *Fig. 10.7. From top to bottom. The hatched lines seen on the*
reverse of inscribed bobbins. "Esther". "A Present From My
Father." "James". Typically two of these bobbins made by Jesse are
missing the top of the head.

It is ironic that the poor state of the pewter which is such a distinctive feature of most of the surviving bobbins, was due to using high quality material, rather than being caused by using cheaper, inferior qualities which one might have expected to have had a shorter life.

One or two of Jesse's pewter inlaid bobbins have survived

"Suckess to the Pillow Lace" might possibly be an election bobbin handed out by a candidate as a gift to encourage the recipient to vote in his favour. Jesse certainly made election bobbins, one inscribed "Althorp and Milton" is in the collection of bobbins at Bedford Museum.

The most important part of his bobbins was the inscription, decoration was kept to a minimum and usually consisted of two or three coloured grooves at each end of the shank.

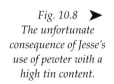

Fig. 10.8 ▶
The unfortunate
consequence of Jesse's
use of pewter with a
high tin content.

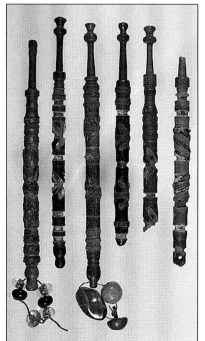

Jesse Compton was also responsible for making some very distinctive bobbins which he decorated with pewter inlay. In the 1981 edition of our book we referred to these bobbins as being the work of "Maker B" but on careful and close inspection of heads, tails and the inscriptions on many of the pewter inlaid bobbins, it is clear that this is Jesse's work. Unfortunately the pewter which Jesse used has corroded very badly because he used a good quality pewter which had an appropriately high tin content. On analysis we found that 78% of the pewter he used was tin, 20% was

◄ Fig. 10.9.
Bone bobbins
inlaid with
more "rotten"
pewter. Note
the "bistre"
dyed heads on
Nos. 1, 4 & 5.

bobbins this may also show evidence of the bistre dye colouring.

The named bobbins with pewter band decoration often have very fine incised lines separating each letter. The letters themselves are coloured alternately red and green, as are the grooves of three diagonal slashes which appear on the reverse. Several pewter rings decorate the shank on either side of the name with more incised lines between the pewter bands.

Jesse died on 14th January 1857, his will dated 1849 states that he was a turner.

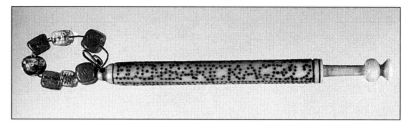

▲ Fig. 10.10. The inscribed bobbin above reads,
"Anthony Yeats Died March 14 1831 Berid March 13 (?) At Weeden Barick Age 22."

in better condition. There is one in Bedford Museum with all its pewter intact with a beautiful shine to its inlaid decoration. Perhaps the pewter used on this bobbin was not of such a high quality or perhaps the bobbin was just not used so much, but whatever the cause, bobbins such as these are the exception rather than the rule.

It is particularly unfortunate that so many of Jesse's bobbins should have deteriorated so badly, as his patterns of inlay are some of the most complex and attractive of any bobbins decorated in this way. His spirals flow evenly and fluently in both directions, and his Butterfly bobbins frequently have as many as nine pewter bands separating the two rows of butterflies which may have up to five pairs of "wings".

Jesse Compton

▲ Jesse Compton's signature taken from his last
will and testament dated 19th May 1849.

He used both wood and bone for his pewter inlaid work and it is the bone bobbins which bear a second very distinctive feature, as he frequently dyed the top part of the bobbin a soft-bistre shade, which although it may not be so evident on the head, is generally more obvious on the long neck which has been protected from the light by the thread.

Both wooden and bone pewter inlaid bobbins bear a third distinguishing feature which is unique to this work. Above the last band of pewter at the top of the shank Jesse adds a small piece of turned decoration by cutting two quite clean deep grooves into the otherwise even thickness of the shank, leaving a very fine ridge between the two. On bone

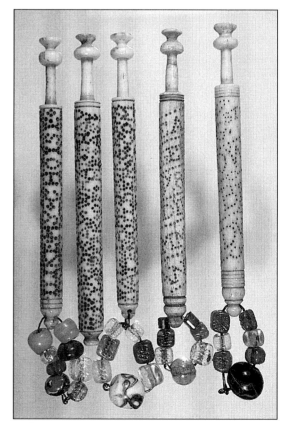

▲ Fig. 10.11. Inscribed bobbins from left to right.
"My Mind Is Fixed Know No More To Range
I Like My Choise To Well To Change."
"When This You See Remember Me And Bear Me In Your Mind
Let All The World Say What Thay Will
Speek Of Me As You Find 26 May 1841."
"William Dockery Private Soilder Y Company Of The
1 Batalion Of The Granideir Gaurds 1849."
"Ann Hammond Died Feby 8 1834 Aged 70 Years."
"Edwin Benbow August 1839."

James Compton
1824 – 1889

His father taught him his skills well, and James made a variety of neatly inscribed bobbins as well as a number of decoratively turned bobbins both in bone and wood. Some of these bobbins have wire wrapped decoration, others have beaded shanks, but we have seen none so far that have been inlaid with pewter, which is unusual for he must have seen his father producing that style of bobbin.

▲ Fig. 11.1. A typical head and tail shape from a
James Compton bobbin.

James was the eldest of Jesse's six children. He was married on December 26th 1845 and judging by the confidence of his signature he was obviously literate, but his wife was not able to sign her own name. They had six children, although James, their youngest son died before he was three weeks old. Perhaps it was considered more important for the girls to be skilled at lace-making, but neither of their two daughters were able to sign their name on their marriage lines, whereas their brothers seemed to be much more competent with pen and pencil.

Unlike his father who rarely described himself officially as a bobbin maker, James consistently declared himself to be either a turner or a bobbin maker for his entire working life. In some ways this is rather surprising, as we would have expected his father Jesse to have been in a better position to have made his living by making bobbins, whereas James, living and working at a time when lacemaking was beginning to decline might have found it harder to support his family from bobbin making alone.

Certainly James does not appear to have made the same quantity of spiral inscriptions bearing general mottoes as his father, the bulk of his inscriptions being commissioned to record specific family events. Many of these were ordered by lacemakers in the Buckingham area, as James regularly walked the seven miles from Deanshanger to Buckingham to sell his bobbins. It is said that for a wager, James once drank a pint of beer in "The Beehive", Deanshanger and then walked to Buckingham where he drank a second pint, all in the space of one hour.

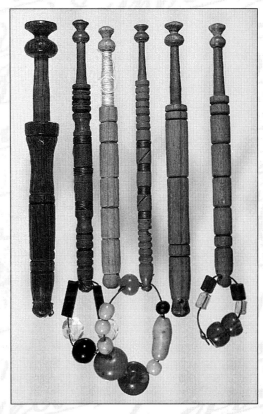

▲ Fig. 11.3. Plainly turned wood bobbins.

James produced a large number of plainly turned bobbins in pale woods all neatly turned with incised bands, sometimes these bands were coloured with blue, red or yellow.

The heads of his bobbins have a tapered long neck and squashed bulb rather similar to those of his father, but the short neck is thicker, and there is not such a sharp division between the bulb and the top section of the head, which was such a weak point in Jesse's bobbins. James used the same flaring rim and neatly turned off the top surface.

The tails of his bobbins are also rather different from those of his father. James sloped the end of the shank in towards a much larger "knob". Sometimes this slope is even slightly concave.

▲ Fig. 11.2. The Beehive pub at Deanshanger.

▲ Fig. 11.4. Left to right.
"Jane". "If You Love Me Be True To Me".
"Aunt Smith Died At Padbury Nov 9 1875".
"When This You See Remember Me J Roberts". "Be True".
Note the style of lettering on these inscribed bobbins.

minister), Alma, (to commemorate part of the Crimean campaign), all appeared on his bobbins. These were most probably made as stock, whereas the name "Jane" might well have been made as an ordered bobbin. Both of these styles, the loose spiral and the tighter form were made in wood and bone, although wooden bobbins with the solid spiral line are much less common than the same form in bone.

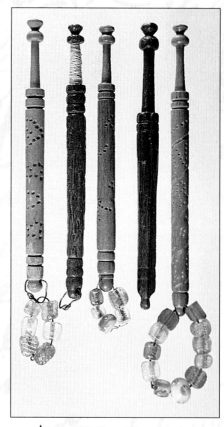

▲ Fig. 11.5. From left to right.
"Rob" (with heart). An illegible oak inscribed
bobbin. "Prince". The famous "Wakes Oak".
"Love Your Love".

On the whole James's bobbins were much larger and thicker than those of his father's. There are several fat bone bobbins which have been inscribed with up to four lines of horizontal lettering and all the words are completely legible. His larger bobbins were probably better suited to the coarser thread used for the much heavier Bedfordshire lace which was perhaps more widespread than the finer Point lace which had been so widely made in his father's day.

James made two styles of spiral inscription. One was very similar to that of his father, with a solid line spiralling up the bobbin in a right handed spiral direction. The other has a very much looser spiral without any such line. This allowed him to fill the shank with a very much shorter motto or name. Such names as Victoria (the Queen), Gladstone (the prime

His horizontal inscriptions were worked on both wood and bone, and like the spiral inscriptions, had the very minimum of decoration, perhaps just one or two coloured lines at each end of the shank.

The lettering is always neatly executed with serifs at the end of the upright lines in such letters as I, J and T. The letter Y is written with a curling stem, and the letter W is made up of two overlapping V's. His figure ones also had a horizontal serif at both top and bottom, but most distinctive of all is

This Marriage
was
solemnized
between us,
{ *James Compton*
Elizabeth Andrews ✕

▲ *The signature of James Compton and his wife's mark on*
their marriage lines dated 26th December 1845.

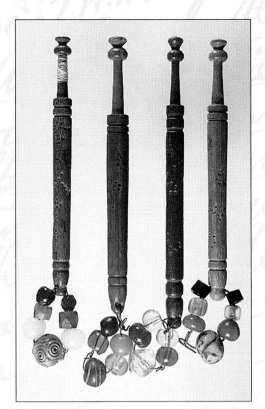

Fig. 11.6. Loose wooden spiral inscriptions,
from left to right.
"Arthur". "Punch". Gladston". "Jesus".

and demonstrates that he was prepared to accept a variety of commissions and sometimes used similar forms of decoration.

A truly prolific pair of bobbin makers.

Together, the bobbin making careers of Jesse and James Compton spanned the greater part of the nineteenth century, from the more prosperous period for lacemaking at the beginning of the century, to the years of decline towards its close. They produced a tremendous quantity of bobbins, specialising in the spiral inscription, which relatively few bobbin makers mastered to the same degree. To give some idea of the proportion of bobbins they made, we examined and identified all of the spirally inscribed bobbins on permanent display in Luton Museum in 1980. Of the seventy three, seven were the distinctive left-hand spiral of Bobbin Brown, five are the work of a maker as yet unidentified, and no less than sixty one were made by the Comptons with Jesse being responsible for rather more than half of these. A truly prolific pair of bobbin makers.

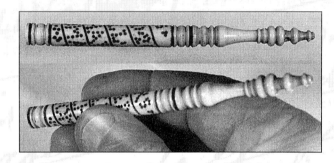

Fig. 11.7 & 11.8. A bone pen handle made by James Compton.
The inscription reads, "Thomas Chappell Aged 21 Years".

the omission of the top line of the figure five. All these features can be clearly seen on the bobbins in the photographs. The letters are coloured alternately red and blue, and sometimes the words are separated by four dots arranged in a diamond shape, or by two dots one above the other like a colon. The Reverend Roberts told Thomas Wright that these dots were made by a drill, then powdered colours mixed with the best gum Arabic were applied using a crow quill with a kind of "twirling motion". The bobbins were placed upright in a rack until the paint was dry. Thomas Wright suggests that some of James's father's bobbins were coloured in with green and chrome yellow, but we have found no surviving examples, however we have seen a number of inscribed wooden bobbins made by James using red and yellow colouring.

One most unusual piece of work that we have seen is a bone pen handle with the inscription "Thomas Chappell Aged 21 Years." When we purchased this piece the portion upon which the metal knib holder fitted had been sawn off and a bobbin head and neck had been crudely attached. It is unmistakably the work of James

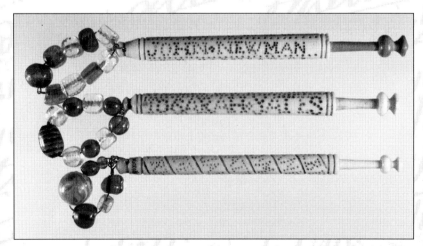

Fig. 11.9. Bone inscriptions by James Compton.
Top, "John Newman Died Januar 21 1849 Aged 40 Years".
Middle, "A Present From William Yates To Sarah Yates".
Bottom, "A Present From Jane Yates To Maryann Webb".
(Courtesy of Northampton Museum and Art Gallery.")

29

Joseph, David & Robert Haskins

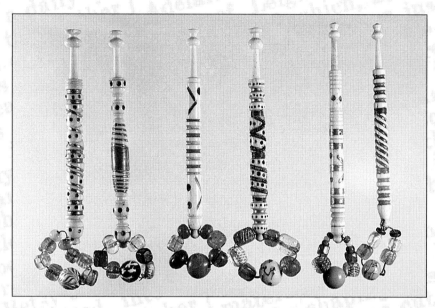

▲ *Fig. 12.1. From left to right.*
Two bobbins made by Joseph Haskins. Two bobbins made by David Haskins.
Two bobbins made by Robert Haskins.

Using the method of grouping bobbins with the same heads, tails and distinctive features we had noted a family of bobbins clearly made by the same hand. They were of exceptional quality, head and shoulders above other bobbins made in the last century.

Looking more closely at this collection it was clear that although the styles and influences were similar throughout, it could be subdivided into three distinct branches.

The bobbins in the first group were of extremely high quality, but the overall shaping of the head is more compressed than the rounded and elongated shape of the second group. The materials used, the fine detail, the outstanding design and skilful execution all indicate a gifted and experienced bobbinmaker's work. Even the baby bobbins inside the mother and babe bobbins are decorated, a feature not seen in other turners' work. Many of the bobbins are highly decorated with tinsel, beads, coloured spots, loose rings, inlaid turquoise stones and even real gold leaf. This group of bobbins contained the election bobbin "Robinson For Ever" which together with other dateable bobbins indicated that they were made at the beginning of the nineteenth century.

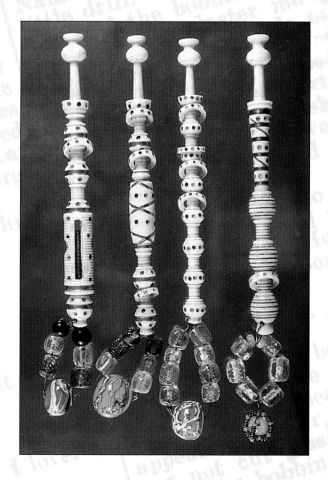

Fig. 12.2. Magnificent bone bobbins with loose rings, ▶
wire and gold leaf decoration.

The second division of bobbins also contained beautifully made and lavishly decorated bobbins. Again the tiny bobbins inside the mother and babe bobbins were carefully worked and gold leaf was used to decorate the more elaborate styles. This sub group is clearly defined by its head shape, which is more open than the first with a distinctive flared trumpet bell forming the small neck and top.

The third division is a shadow of the previous two. The head shape is similar, but less well de-fined, being thicker and heavier. The bobbins lack style although they are of reasonable quality.

The similarities between the three groups suggested a common influence and we began to look for a related group of bobbinmakers who might have made these bobbins. As they had produced such quality and quantity they must have been well known. We felt that through our researches we

▼ Fig. 12.4. Four of Joseph's less extravagantly decorated bone bobbins, and on the right "Robinson For Ever".

▲ Fig. 12.3. Splendid bone bobbins with loose rings and gold leaf decoration.

must have discovered their names without being able to link those names to specific bobbins. The following article from "The Bedfordshire Times" & "The Independent" of May 19th 1912 allowed us to make the connection. We are grateful to "The Bedfordshire Times" for permission to publish the following extract which tells us a great deal about the bobbin makers in the Haskins family.

"How Bobbins Were Made"

"Since the first part of this article appeared, we have received some interesting information from Mr R Haskins, Stanley Street, who comes from a family of bobbin makers. His grandfather made bobbins in St John's, and afterwards in St Peter's in a cottage opposite the Rectory. Bob, before he was 15 years of age, used to saw the bones, and he has specimens of his own turning. He can distinguish anywhere bobbins that were made by his family. Wooden bobbins were made by a Mr Abbott, who lived in Foster Hill Road, and the wood employed was either Cherry or plum-tree, mostly the latter. Another maker of wooden bobbins was George Lumbis of Renhold. Bob's father also made spangles, including the bottom beads, in St John's and in Adelaide square. His uncle David Haskins, of Leighton Buzzard, also made bobbins, one of which, at least 80 years old, was produced for our inspection. It is certainly quite unique, the shank being of the open work styled "church-window" bobbins, but containing in it two tiny bobbins, one inside the other – in all, therefore three bobbins. Each tiny bobbin is neatly turned and coloured with red and blue spots. As to how these got one inside the other, Mr Haskins explained that the bone was more flexible when fresh, and it was not difficult to widen the openings. Shin bone was the material used for bobbins, and practically all the shaping was done in the lathe, and the open-work was cut with a fine circular saw. Names and mottoes were dotted in with a little drill. Lead was the metal with which many of the bobbins were mounted, it was applied in a plaster mould and turned off in the lathe afterwards to make it smooth. When wire was twined on for ornament it was fixed in the holes drilled for the purpose. It was considered important, says Mr Haskins, that the bobbins should have a smooth surface, and carved work should be objectionable as it irritated the fingers in working.

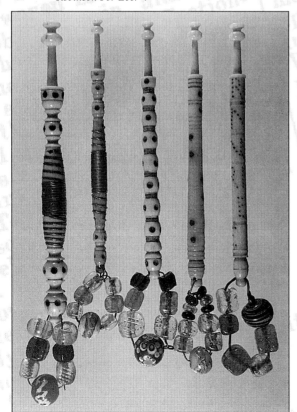

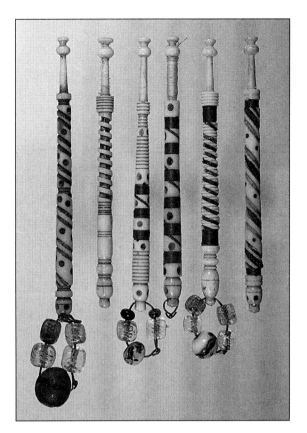

▼ *Fig. 12.5. Six bone bobbins which are nicely turned and decorated.*

he declares that the making of bottom beads is not a lost art, and he could take it up tomorrow, or show anyone how to do it. The glass was obtained from decanter tops, and tallow lamps were used for melting it. Colouring matter was obtained from London."

Joseph Haskins was born in 1779 and is first mentioned in the 1830 Trade Directory as a bead and bobbin maker in St John's, Bedford. Nine years later he is listed as a lapidary and bead maker in Ampthill Street, Bedford. He died in Bedford in 1855 at the age of seventy six. His son David was born in 1819, and later moved to Leighton Buzzard where he carried on his father's trade. Robert Haskins and Robert Richard Haskins are recorded as "working jeweller" and "working silversmith" in the Trade Directories published between 1850 and 1894, so clearly fine craftsmanship ran in the family.

Looking again at the "family" of bobbins described above and the information from "The Bedfordshire Times & Independent" we began to compare the bobbins with the description from the newspaper. We could clearly see the work of three independent but closely linked bobbin makers whose production appeared to span three generations from the start through to the end of the 1800's. We noted that the first two bobbin makers decorated the baby bobbin which they fitted inside their mother and babe bobbin. We have found no other bobbin makers who went to such lengths. Added to this, these bobbin makers also used gold leaf and one actually inlaid turquoise stones into a bobbin suggesting a link with the jewellery and lapidary trade. We would therefore suggest that these bobbins are the work of Joseph, David and Robert Haskins.

Joseph Haskins 1779 – 1855

Joseph Haskins produced some of the finest and most elaborate bobbins of the last century. They were lavishly decorated with beads, pewter, wire, tinsel, gold leaf, loose

Mr Haskins used to sell bobbins regularly at Bedford Fair, and made them himself up to the year 1851. He produced one of bone which he made. Some bobbins would fetch a shilling each.

They were of exceptional quality,

head and shoulders above other bobbins

made in the last century

The bead maker says Mr Haskins, was called a lapidary. He spurns the idea that the old English beads were made in Germany, though he has no doubt that some of the modern beads come from abroad. It appears, however, that the so-called "cuts" are not cut glass. Attached to the above described bobbin was a very typical spangle, with "cuts" and bottom bead identical with those we saw at Kempston. These beads, he says, were melted off one at a time, from a stick of glass and twirled on a copper wire which made the hole, then pressed on the sides with a file which produced at once the square shape and the peculiar markings on the surface. The bottom bead was also made on a wire. The specimen before us is of opalescent glass, and Mr Haskins says the colour was dotted in while the glass was soft. At all events,

▲ *Fig. 12.6. Typical head and tail shapes turned by Joseph Haskins.*

rings, coloured spots and grooves. It must have been a rare pleasure for a lace maker to see one of these beautiful bone bobbins shining out amongst so many plainer bobbins on her pillow.

> *A favourite design of this craftsman*
>
> *was to pierce the lower half*
>
> *of the shank for a babe*

He made a great quantity of bobbins, so examples of his work are easy to find. Many of his best bobbins, particularly the mother and babes, and bone bobbins decorated with loose rings have found their way into museum collections, and because they are of such superlative quality a large number are to be seen on permanent display. Luton Museum have a particularly magnificent collection of these highly decorated bobbins which is really well worth seeing.

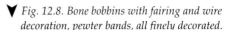

▼ Fig. 12.8. Bone bobbins with fairing and wire decoration, pewter bands, all finely decorated.

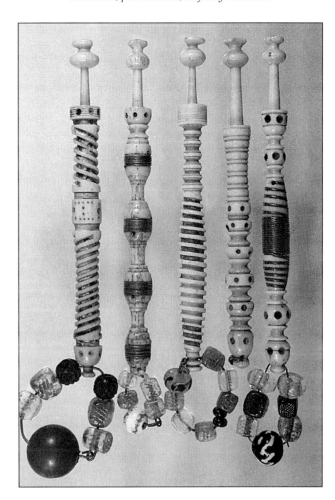

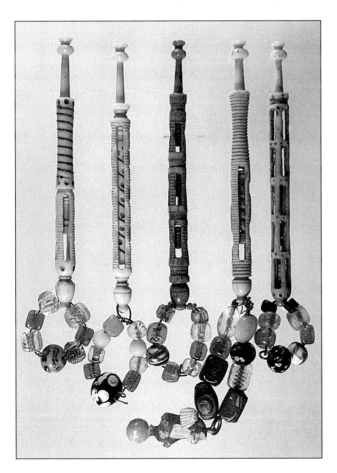

▲ Fig. 12.7. Above. Bone mother and babe bobbins. Note the decorated babes.

Fig. 12.9. Bone bobbin with inlaid turquoise stone. ➤

His most elaborate bobbins are easily identified, but he also made a lot of bobbins with far less decoration which would have been much less expensive, and therefore within the pocket of a greater number of lace-makers. These relatively plainer styles are therefore more common than his lavishly decorated examples.

Joseph was definitely making bobbins during the earlier part of the nineteenth century because he made a bone bobbin inscribed "Robinson For Ever". This referred to Sir George Robinson who stood for Northampton Borough in the five Parliamentary elections between 1818 and 1832. It would have been during one of these campaigns that such bobbins would have been commissioned and given away as inducements to vote for Robinson.

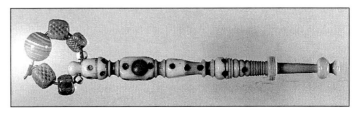

Joseph arranged the lettering of this election slogan in a very unusual way. In fact we have only seen one other bobbin where the words have been split up and inscribed in syllables in layers around the bobbin.

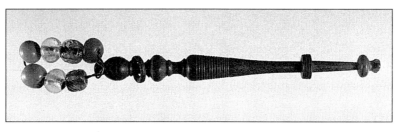
▲ *Fig. 12.10. A wooden loose ring bobbin.*
(Courtesy of Northampton Museum and Art Gallery.)

mother and babes, is the group of closely spaced, lightly incised lines which he marks on the shank before cutting the window slits. The bars of bone remaining between each slit are often given additional shaping.

It is the distinctive tail end of the bobbin that has enabled us to identify several more types of bobbin which were made by the same craftsman. He often finished his bobbins with a round or oval shaped "bead" which has one line incised around its widest part. There is a neat little projection under this oval or round, which is drilled to take the spangle.

The shape of the head of the bobbin will confirm the work of this maker. It has a rather squashed bulb, surmounted by a very triangular top section. The top surface of the rim is usually quite flat, not turned or shaped at all. Because this is not the usual practice of bobbin makers, it is important to look for.

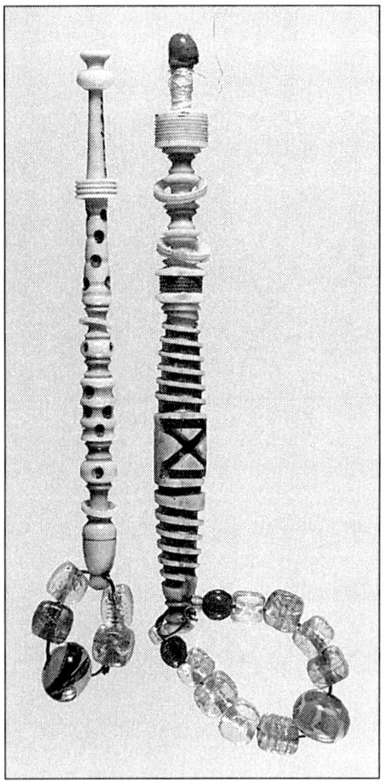

He seems to have had two ways of shaping the shank, some quite straight, others being neatly tapered beneath a distinctly ridged collar.

His most notable work must surely be his "luxury" bobbins. A good many of this type of bobbin features at least one compartment containing a baby bobbin, and some have as many as four such compartments in the length of the shank. His "piece de resistance" in this style must be the superb example in Luton Museum which has no less than 18 little alcoves made in the shank, each containing a tiny green bobbin held in place with a spiralling strand of brass wire. Even the babes he added to his bobbins were usually decorated with a spiral groove which he coloured or filled with a strip of tinsel. Occasionally the baby bobbins may be made from lead or pewter. A further interesting detail which distinguishes his

A favourite design of this craftsman was to pierce the lower half of the shank for a babe, and then to add very elaborate decoration to the upper part. This might take the form of pewter inlay, tiny beads, strips of tinsel, or even a combination of these last two.

It must have been a rare pleasure

for a lace maker to see one

of these beautiful bone bobbins

Joseph used a lot of tinsel in his designs. Sometimes this was in the form of thin sheet metal in various colours, the ends of which needed to be bound in place with brass wire. This has tended to tarnish over the years and is rarely as

▲ *Fig. 12.11. A pair of bone bobbins with loose rings.*
(Courtesy of Northampton Museum and Art Gallery.)

▲ *Fig. 12.12. Beautifully turned wooden bobbins, some as originally intended having no spangle hole.*

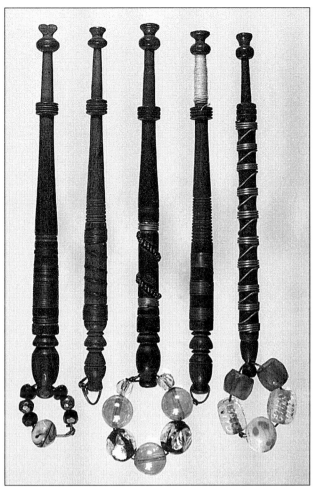

◀ *Fig. 12.13. Wire decorated wooden bobbins.*

▼ *Fig. 12.15. Pewter inlaid wooden bobbins.*

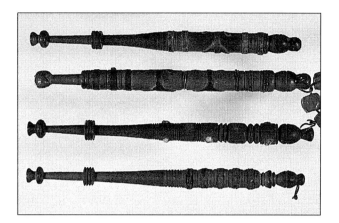

fill bands turned into the bobbin around the shank, in much the same way as he used colour on his cheaper bobbins. However, because it was not held in with wire, nor was the gold leaf in this case applied directly, much of this form of decoration has come loose with wear, and a large proportion is now missing from his bobbins. Where it has survived it still has its original bright colouring, giving these bobbins a truly outstanding appearance.

Many other bobbin makers had sufficient skill to produce mother and babes, but very few had the high degree of skill needed to turn bobbins with loose rings in bone. Joseph produced this style in considerable quantity, but unfortunately the rings were fragile and many have not survived. Those bobbins which do retain some of their rings show that in many cases the rings were decorated with coloured spots or gold leaf. This would have been done before the rings were turned free of the shank. Some of the thicker bobbins he made, had as many as seven loose rings spaced at regular intervals down the shank. The spaces between each ring were embellished with pewter bands, spots, rows of tiny beads, pierced windows for mother and babes or coloured bands.

bright in appearance as the glittering gold leaf, which he used to such good effect on so many bobbins. Some of this gold leaf was laid on paper and was probably a lot easier to use than the tinsel for it would be far more flexible than the thin metal sheet. It would follow the bottom of the spiral channels made to accommodate it very closely. This reveals that the channel was made with a small file, the bobbin being turned in the lathe by hand as the work on the groove progressed, leaving behind a channel with a series of flat surfaces forming the bottom of the groove. Because some of this paper backed gold leaf was held in place with glue, it could be used to

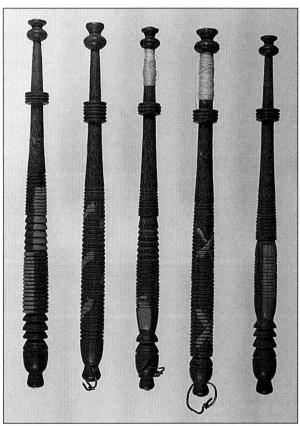

Fig. 12.14. ▶
Wooden bitted bobbins.

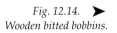

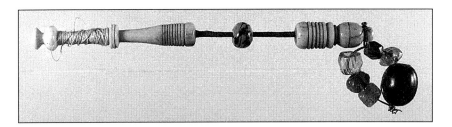

We have seen several bone fairings of his, two of which retained their original tinsel in remarkably bright condition. Unfortunately the tiny strips were often glued into the groove, rather than being held in place with brass wire, and much of the tinsel is missing from these bobbins. These fairings generally have a group of closely spaced lines incised at the top of the shank, very similar to those on the collar of his tapered bobbins.

Some bobbins which Joseph made were notably "chunky" being almost twice the diameter of some of his slimmer versions. These two very different sizes of bobbin can also be seen amongst those that he decorated with brass wire. These bands of wire were connected with saw cuts made diagonally in a left handed spiral direction. The spiral grooves of his fairings were also made in the same direction, which makes it a point worth looking out for when trying to identify the work of this maker.

He also made finely turned small wooden bobbins ornamented with most attractive patterns of ridges and hollows. These have a nicely tapered shank and the distinctively ridged collar, but not all were intended to be spangled as many

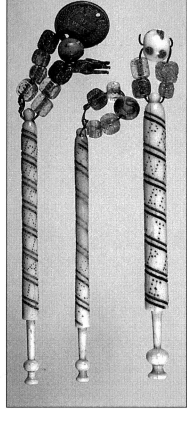

▲ *Fig. 12.16. What remains of a beaded shank bobbin. (Courtesy of Northampton Museum and Art Gallery.)*

Fig. 12.17. From left to right. ▶
" How Hard To Love And Not Be Love Again."
"A Present — — — — — Gurney."
"A Present For Elizabeth Spencer."
The bobbins need to be held 'upside down' to be read.

▼ *Fig. 12.18. Wire decorated bone bobbins.*

have no hole drilled for this purpose, they were obviously intended for use in making the finer Buckinghamshire Point lace.

It was not just fine turning which Joseph applied to wooden bobbins, he treated wood to a similar decorative excess using pewter inlay, wire, tinsel, beads, bitted decoration, loose rings, but as yet we have not seen a mother and babe style wooden bobbin which he made.

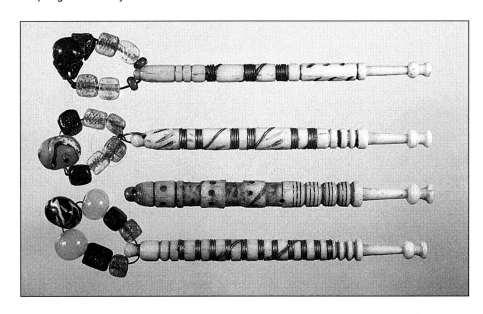

There is one particularly interesting bobbin in the Northampton Museum collection which shows very clearly how a bobbin with a bead shank was constructed, as unfortunately only one of the glass beads remains on the length of wire which connects the two bone sections of the shank. It is quite a rare design and must have been a beautiful bobbin when it was first made.

The points to look for when identifying Joseph's work are the shaping at the end of the shank, the completely flat surface of the top of the rim, and the heavily ridged collar of his tapered bobbins. His fatter bobbins are particularly distinctive.

The overall length of many of his shanks shows a slight tapering towards the head. In some of his better quality bobbins particularly the slimmer, smaller examples, this taper is more pronounced, leading up to a collar or cup-shape which is often decorated with incised lines, yet more spots, or a combination of both.

In our opinion Joseph Haskins was the most skilful craftsman producing decorated lace bobbins during the nineteenth century. His designs and his ability to turn them into such beautiful bobbins put him in a class of his own. He produced, not just one or two out-standing bobbins, but a whole series of masterpieces, which must be the envy of today's bobbin maker and lacemaker alike.

The few spirally inscribed bobbins made by Joseph are unusual for they read upside down. They are lefthand spirals, usually with two lines of decoration spiralling up the bobbin. The bobbins are arranged in the photograph so that they may be read more easily.

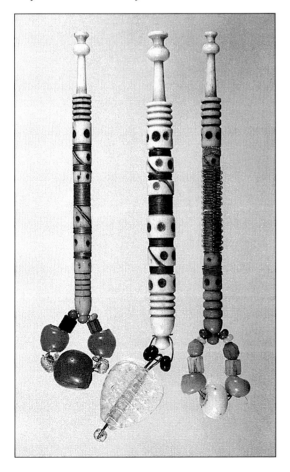

▲ *Fig. 13.1. Head and tail made by David Haskins.*

David Haskins 1819 –

The style of decoration will give the first clue to identification of David's work, and a closer look at the shape of the head and tail will give confirmation, as both are distinctive. The long neck is quite tapered and the bulb is very generous in diameter and looks as if it has been compressed downwards, giving a slightly squashed appearance. The short neck is surprisingly tall, suddenly flaring out at the top like a trumpet bell with a most distinctive rim which is quite flat on the top and often shows evidence of saw marks left when the piece of bone was originally cut to length.

The end of the bobbin is neatly rounded into a cup shape standing on a stem, which is drilled to take the spangle. Very often the " bowl" of the cup is decorated with incised lines and spots and slashes to match the decoration on the shank.

The styles of decoration which David used are extremely varied. We have seen few of his bone bobbins which rely solely on ornamental turning to decorate the shank, he much preferred to add a series of coloured bands to each end of the shank and then fill in the space between with bands of brass wire. These bands were always linked with a groove running in a left handed spiral direction. Sometimes a spiral of tinsel filled the main part of the shank, on other bobbins tiny beads were added in criss-cross or spiral grooves. He also added diagonal slashes and large spots to the shanks, frequently these were combined with wire binding. The grooves, spots or slashes on his bobbins always seem to be filled with red or blue colouring.

◄ *Fig. 13.2. Wire and bead decorated bobbins. The middle bobbin is most typical of David's work.*

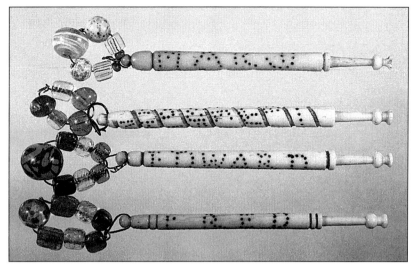

◄ Fig. 13.3. Left, from top to bottom.
"Mary".
"M — — — — — Johnson Faseley 1863".
"Edward".
"Fred".
Note the long curving tail of the
"Y" in the name Mary.

▼ Fig. 13.4. Below, from left to right.
"Robert Franklin Helmdon 1846."
"John Smith Is Dead And Gone."
"Benjamin Mallard Blisworth Northamptonshire."
(Courtesy Of Northampton Museum
and Art Gallery.)

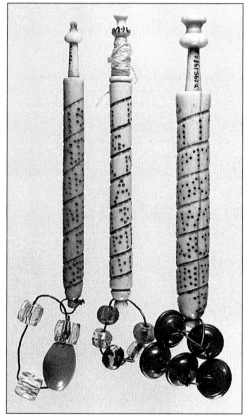

The short neck is surprisingly tall,

suddenly flaring out at the top like a

trumpet bell with a most distinctive rim

We have found a number of named bobbins made by David and they are extremely simple, with the name in large capitals on one side and two rows of staggered dots on the other. The colouring on these named bobbins is always red and blue. His lettering was very plain and straightforward, with no extra dots at the end of his straight lines. His "Y's" he writes with a long, curving tail, as can be seen from the bobbin inscribed "Mary" in the photograph. He sometimes added a name to some of his more elaborately decorated bobbins, very often in spiral form on the centre part of the shank with mother and babe compartments at each end. This spiral sometimes followed a right handed direction which we find unusual for most of his other spirals are made in a left handed direction. On the whole inscribed bobbins do not seem to have been his forte.

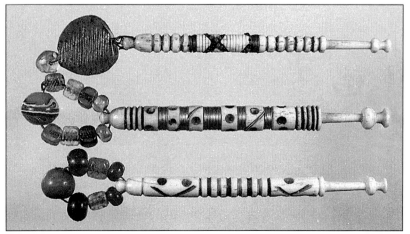

◄ Fig. 13.5. Three typically decorated bone
bobbins by David Haskins.

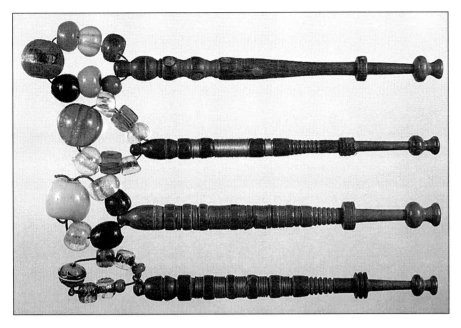

Fig. 13.6. A pewter Leopard above three wire decorated bobbins. All made of wood.

Fig. 13.7. A pewter butterfly in bone and a wooden wire decorated bobbin.

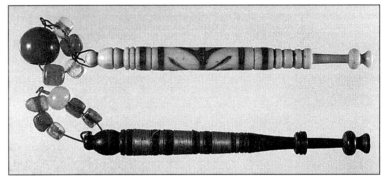

David produced a good number of nicely turned and decorated wood bobbins, well proportioned, but a little heavier than those produced by his father Joseph. Although he employed the more usual form of decoration on these wooden bobbins, wire, tinsel and pewter, David occasionally produced a bobbin decorated with brass pins. On close inspection of what might appear a plain wood bobbin, tiny dull dots can be seen on the bobbin body. A careful rub with a gentle abrasive will bring these dull spots to brilliant sparkling gold pin pricks turning a mediocre wood bobbin into a dazzling delight.

David was well taught by his father. Many of his more elaborate bone bobbins are excellent in design and execution, but his range and variety of work cannot compare with Joseph's output, perhaps the demand for bobbins had peaked in his father's time, but even so the standard of David's work still sets him well above most bobbin makers of his time.

Fig. 13.9.
David Haskins at his best, two mother and babe bobbins and a splendid beaded bobbin.

Fig. 13.8. A brass pin inlaid bobbin, the pins can just be seen glittering.

◀ *Fig. 14.1. Head and tail shapes which Robert Haskins produced.*

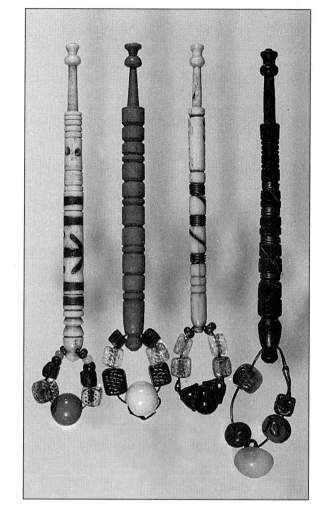

Robert Haskins

Identifying Robert's work is relatively simple. The heads and tails resemble those produced by his uncle David, but they are much less well defined, being plumper, thicker and rather lacking in character. The range of decoration tends to be limited to wire, coloured slashes and dots with occasional use of pewter inlay (which is of good quality). He produced bobbins in both wood and bone but although they are reasonably well made they lack the flair which his uncle and grandfather had in such abundance.

However it is important to remember that Robert was making and selling bobbins, during the latter part of the nineteenth century. Lacemaking was in decline at this time, so demand for new bobbins was small. This lack of demand would give Robert neither the bobbin making skill through practice and repetition nor the encouragement to make more elaborate bobbins which he might not even be able to sell. It is therefore understandable that the bobbins he produced were less inspiring than those of his grandfather and uncle.

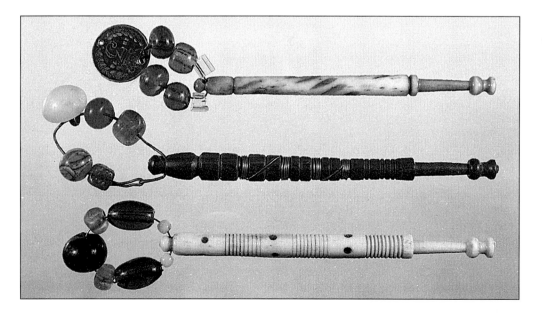

▲
◀ *Fig. 14.2 & 14.3.
Left and above.
Typical examples of
Robert Haskins' work.*

Bobbin Brown of Cranfield
1793 – 1872

The censuses of 1841, 1851 and 1861 reveal that there was only one man by the name of Brown who could possibly be the "Bobbin Brown of Cranfield" referred to in Thomas Wright's book and so many subsequent publications. William Brown of Tartlett End, Cranfield describes himself as a bobbin maker in all three censuses and is one of the very few men to record bobbin making as their primary occupation. Most called themselves labourers or woodturners.

▲ *Fig. 15.1. Head and tail turned by "Bobbin" Brown.*

William Brown was the eldest child of James and Alice Brown. He was born in Cranfield and was christened there on 9th June 1793. He had no less than nine younger brothers and sisters. William himself had six children by his first wife, Sarah, although their eldest child died when he was only nine months old. Unfortunately we have been unable to find any record of Bobbin Brown's marriage. This is very disappointing as it would have been interesting to know if he was able to sign his marriage lines, or if he could only make his mark, as so many people of that time were illiterate.

---

the lettering on the bobbins

produced by this maker is "unmistakable,

spiral, bold and very neat"

Sarah died in 1847 and on the census four years later William is described as a widower living with Mary Hannah, his unmarried daughter, and her month old daughter. By 1857, at the age of sixty-four he is married again, to Hannah, a lacemaker twenty years his junior, who bears him two sons. Again we have not been able to find any record of William's and Hannah's marriage, although their elder son George was married in Cranfield at the age of twenty-one to one of the village lacemakers and they were both unable to manage more than a shaky X beside their names in the parish records. So it seems that neither William nor his wife had been able to teach their son to write even his own name. This would cast doubt on their own literacy.

There is some evidence to suggest that one of these two sons followed in his father's footsteps, as an elderly resident of Cranfield remembers a "Bobbin Brown" who lived at Tartlett End in the early years of this century. Obviously this could not have been William Brown who died in 1872, but it

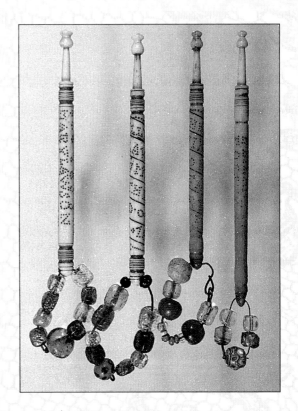

▲ *Fig. 15.2. Above, from left to right.*
"Mary Lawson My Mother Died Dec 31 1853."
" William Lawson My Father D Oct 12 1853."
"John Bavington My Father 1855."
"Elizabeth Fossey My Mother." (Well worn.)
The spiral inscriptions are, as you see,
"bold and very neat."

could well have been George or Jesse. This "Bobbin Brown" is described as "a small fat little fellow who made both quills and bobbins" and is recalled as having a brother called Ginger. Neither of the two were remembered as being about when this person returned from the Great War. In fact, both George and Jesse died before the end of the war – George in 1917 and Jesse in the following year. Unfortunately, to the gentleman who remembered the younger Bobbin Brown, one bobbin looked much like another, so it is hardly surprising that, from this source, we were not able to find out which bobbins he made.

It was amongst the bobbins in the J S Elliott collection in Bedford Museum that we found one which was labelled as being made in Cranfield. Steele-Elliott had kept a notebook in which he listed his bobbins and in some instances he added further details, and it is here that a most distinctive bone bobbin with a spiral inscription is recorded as having been made at Cranfield.

Thomas Wright gives the following description of Bobbin Brown's work, "Brown was unmistakable, being spiral, bold and very neat". With this description in mind we took a closer look at the bobbin in Bedford Museum. It is extremely unusual, with a left-hand spiral in which the inscription starts from the top and reads downwards towards the tail end of the bobbin. Although the lettering on this particular bobbin is not outstandingly neat, there are other similar bobbins where the lettering is quite superlative. The lettering on the bobbins is always in red, as is the spiral line running down the bobbin making the inscription stand out very clearly. So we would certainly consider that the lettering on the bobbins produced by this maker is "unmistakable, spiral, bold and very neat".

Thomas Wright mentioned one other bobbin maker who lived in Cranfield. He was Arthur Wright, the son of the lace pillow maker, but he was not born until 1857 and could not have been responsible for the great number of bobbins we have identified as having been made by the same maker as the Cranfield spiral inscription, because the bulk of these that are dated fall in the 1850s and 60s.

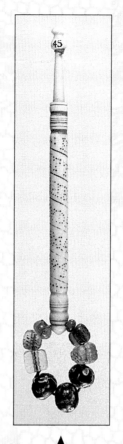

▲

Fig. 15.3. "Harrett Sarah Bird My Dau Born Jan 13 1845." (Courtesy of Bedford Museum.)

The bobbin in the Bedford Museum is inscribed "Harrett Sarah Bird My Dau Bor Jan 13 1845" which would certainly fit in with the dates of Bobbin Brown. He first declared himself to be a bobbin maker on the census of 1841 at the age of 47, and he died in 1872 at the age of 80. So his bobbin making career spanned at least thirty years, and it would have been quite feasible for him to have made all the bobbins dated during the 1850s and 60s.

---

the year before he died

Bobbin Brown describes himself

on the census as a "pauper"

In the course of our researches we have gone through all the census returns for Cranfield in 1841, 51, 61, and 71, and the record of every baptism, marriage and burial in the parish of Cranfield during the nineteenth century, but we have not found any other man who describes himself as a bobbin maker on any occasion. So having carefully considered all the information available to us, we feel justified in concluding that William Brown was indeed "Bobbin Brown" of Cranfield who was responsible for this unique style of spiral inscription and the other styles of bobbins which we have been able to link to it. Quite apart from his distinctive decoration and lettering, there are two parts of the bobbin which indicate very clearly those bobbins made by Bobbin Brown. The first, most immediately obvious, is the tail end which he forms into a very shallow point. This point is usually most distinct and because it is so rare for a tail to be shaped in this way, it is, for us, a reliable guide when identifying bobbins made by this craftsman. There are generally just two incised lines at the base of this point between which he drilled the hole to take the spangle. However, on some of the pewter inlaid bobbins a group of these incised lines may fill the space between the end of the shank and the first band of pewter.

Fig. 15.4. Right. Three bone inscriptions. ➤
"Love Is True In Bedfordshire." "Thats A Joke." "My Love To U My Dear."

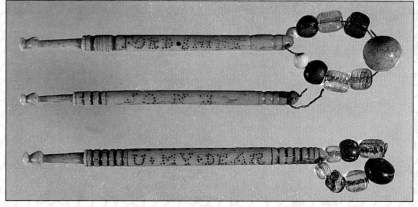

The second distinguishing feature is the shape of the head, and most particularly, the shape of the rim. Most lace bobbins produced by other makers have a flattish top to the rim, but Bobbin Brown's slope down towards the edge of the rim from a very much higher centre, giving an almost dome-like appearance. The shape of the bulb is also distinctive, being fattest immediately above the long neck, and then tapering in to a short neck. This gives a rather bottom-heavy appearance to the bulb, which when combined with the domed top and pointed tail, makes this bobbin maker's work one of the easiest to identify.

If there is still room for doubt after examining the head and tail of the bobbin, then very often the distinctive col-

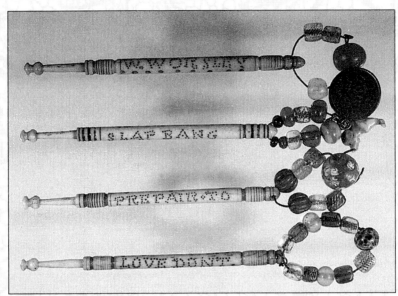

Fig. 15.5. Four special inscriptions made by "Bobbin" Brown. From top to bottom. "W Worsley Hung 1868." "Slap Bang Here We Go Again." "Prepair To Meet Thy God." "Love Don't Be Absent."

ouring of the decoration can confirm its origin. Bobbin Brown used only red, black and yellow for the stripes and spots on his bobbins. On his inscribed bobbins he mainly used two combinations of these three colours. Some bobbins with horizontal lines of lettering have a group of three or five bands at each end of the inscription, these are coloured alternately red and black. Others, with similar horizontal inscriptions and any inscribed in his unique spiral style where the inscription has not been long enough to fill the shank com-

pletely, have a much wider band of yellow (further decorated with a group of incised lines) with a red stripe on each side. This arrangement is repeated on both top and bottom of the shank and can be clearly seen on some of the bobbins

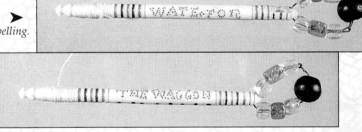

Fig. 15.6 & 15.7. Right. "Wate For The Wagon." A music Hall inscription, such fine writing, such poor spelling.

shown on the colour plate. The William Worsley hanging bobbin of 1868 was decorated in this way. Both groupings of coloured bands can be seen on some of his domino or pewter inlaid bobbins.

He made some very attractive mother and babe bobbins, the most effective of which had one mother and babe compartment at each end of the shank. The plain central area he then inscribed with various romantic sentiments such as "marry or pay what a chance". Again the red, black and yellow stripes are much in evidence.

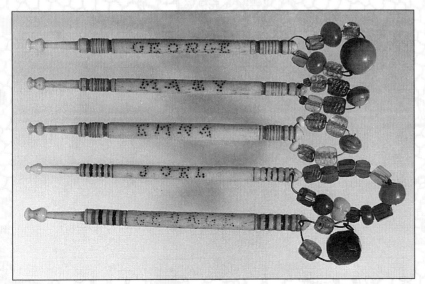

Fig. 15.8. Left, from top to bottom. "George", "Mary", "Emma", "Joel", "George Redman 1864."

The way in which some of the individual letters were formed is also indicative of Bobbin Brown's work. His lettering is surprisingly elaborate with two dots forming a serif at the end of every straight line. This effect can be clearly seen on any of the inscribed bobbins on the photographs. His letter R has a very pronounced upward swing at the end, and the central cross bar of his A and E very often consists of only one dot. The dated bobbins show that he always wrote his figure 1 with the addition of a diagonal line at the top, and two dots form a base line at the bottom. There is also a tendency for his letters to slope slightly forwards, this is most noticeable on the horizontally inscribed bobbins.

His spelling is often very poor, tending to be distinctly phonetic on occasions. This does give rise to some doubts about the extent of his literacy. But in the main, despite some rather erratic spelling, his inscriptions are scrupulously neat. On the reverse side of his named bobbins where there is no date or further lettering to be added, he fills the space with a line of alternate red and black dots, which end in a diamond shaped grouping. This is clearly illustrated on the reverse of the named

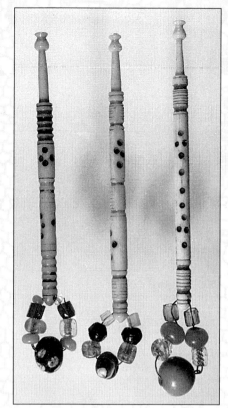

▲ Fig. 15.9. The decoration which appears on the reverse of named bobbins.

bobbin shown in the photograph. Another interesting group of bobbins which he made gives rise to all sorts of speculation. These have a name inscribed on the lower part of the bone shank, which has then been spliced into a wooden top half. One bobbin spliced in this way retains part of the distinct yellow and red banding usually found on the top part of the shank, so this particular bobbin required repair when it's head or neck was damaged in some way. Others show no trace of such previous decoration and might even have been deliberately made in this way in order to use pieces of bone which would otherwise have been too short for a bobbin. In all cases the splice has been very neatly executed and riveted in place by filling two holes drilled through the joint with pewter or with small wooden pegs. Groups of incised lines have then been added to the spliced part of the bobbin.

One of his distinctive spiral inscriptions has been repaired in this manner. We shall probably never know whether this, or similar repairs, became necessary due to wear or damage inflicted by the lacemaker, or whether Bobbin Brown used this as a means of salvaging bobbins whose head or neck broke whilst he was making it. Perhaps he mended it to be used as an extra bobbin for his wife, who would probably not have minded that the inscription was incomplete, as when all is said and done a spliced bobbin makes lace just as well as the most perfect example of the bobbin maker's art. It would have been just as likely then, as it is today, that the bobbin maker's wife had a very large number of "seconds" on her lace pillow.

All the inscribed and decorated bobbins described so far have had a completely regular, unshaped shank, but Bobbin Brown did make two types of bobbins where the shank was shaped. In both cases wooden and bone examples are commonly found.

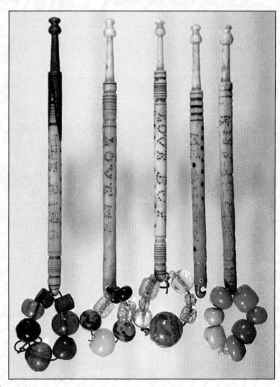

▲ Fig. 15.10. Above, from left to right. A spliced repair "Love Buy The Ring", "Love Me Truley", "Love Buy The Ring", "Mary Me Quick", "Kiss Me Quick."

His spelling is often very poor,

tending to be distinctly

phonetic on occasions

The first type of shaping is quite unique as it gives a rather curious "waisted" effect to the shank. It is generally the top part of the shank which is decorated in this way. A group of incised lines were added at the beginning and end of the shaping, and a third group emphasise the narrowest part in

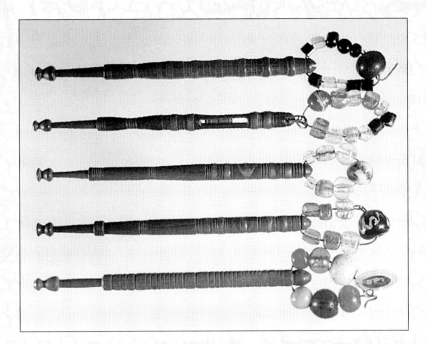

The second, much simpler shaping occurs mainly on those bone and wooden bobbins with pewter decoration. These had quite a long collar decorated with a group of incised lines. The shank then tapers very gradually outwards towards the tail. There are usually several more groups of incised lines on the shank above the pewter work and in between the pewter bands if they are widely spaced.

Clearly Bobbin Brown thoroughly deserved his nick-name. He made an extremely large quantity of quality bobbins in both wood and bone, but it is the neatness of his lettering which makes so many of even the simplest inscribed bone bobbins, really outstanding. Nowadays his bobbins command respectable prices, but in the days when he was making them it was obviously a struggle to earn enough to keep body and soul together. One of his sons died at the age of twenty one in Ampthill Workhouse, and the year before he died Bobbin Brown describes himself on the census as a "pauper". Which is a rather sad note on which to end at least thirty years of bobbin making.

the centre. The remaining two thirds of the shank was then decorated in several ways, the most common being the use of pewter inlay in butterflies, tiger or leopard designs. In some cases a combination of more than one style of inlay has been used to give a very lavish effect.

Bobbin Brown's pewter work remains in excellent condition in both his bone and wooden bobbins, and when well used it develops a shine quite equal to that of silver. Analysis showed that 48% of his pewter consisted of tin and 44% of lead (the remaining proportion was probably Antimony) so this low quality pewter with its correspondingly low tin content, has enabled his bobbins to resist the corrosion which has attacked the work of so many other bobbin makers.

Coloured dots are sometimes added to the tapered parts of the shank above and below the "waist", this is particularly common where the lower part of the shank has been inscribed with names and dates. Coloured stripes may also appear on either side of the inscription.

Luton Museum has a very nicely proportioned mother and babe bobbin in bone, which has this waisted shaping.

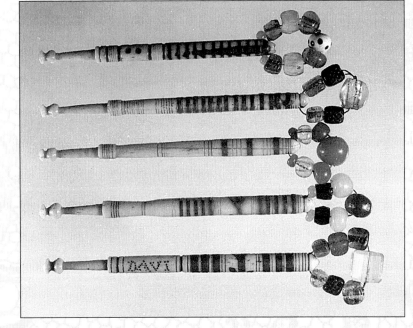

▲ Fig. 15.12. Five pewter inlaid bone bobbins.
Note the "waisted" shaping on the fourth bobbin.

Fig. 15.13. An unusual bone pen handle
made by "Bobbin" Brown, which reads,
"A Gift From His Sister Mary Ann Haynes." ➤

Arthur Wright 1857 – ?

▲ *Fig. 16.1. Head and tail made
by Arthur Wright.*

During the many years in which we have been researching lace bobbins we had noted many, very crudely, inscribed bone bobbins whose heads and tails were very similar to the work of Bobbin Brown. These bobbins had only one red painted band at the top and tail of the shank and an incised line on each side. The lettering, like Bobbin Brown's is always coloured red, but the individual letters are so poorly formed and very erratic that there is little danger of these bobbins being confused with Brown's work. At one time we thought that these bobbins may have been made by Bobbin Brown when his eyesight began deteriorating later in his life, after all we had seen a bobbin of his dated 1871, the year before his death. It is expecting a lot of even the most skilled worker that his lettering at the age of seventy nine should be as perfect as it was thirty years earlier.

The puzzle was solved with the help of two enlightening clues. The first clue was noticing that this particular bobbin maker, when he used spiral wire wrapping as decoration, cut his spiral in a right handed direction, immediately proving to us that this was the work of another turner for, as you will remember, Bobbin Brown was left handed and always cut a left hand spiral. The second, and more interesting, clue came as Christine was looking at various lace pillows during a lace day. Upon one pillow rested a horizontally inscribed bone bobbin made by this "mystery" maker which read "John Bunyan 1874". This bobbin commemorated the raising of a statue to John Bunyan in Bedford square in that year. Bobbin Brown had died in 1872 so there was no possibility that he could have made this particular bobbin. We were now certain that this group of bobbins was the work of someone other than Brown. We next considered why these bobbins looked so similar to Brown's work. It would seem most likely that this bobbin maker had been taught by William Brown, for in the same way that when David teaches someone to make bobbins they produce the same head shape, tail shape and decoration upon the shank, Brown's pupil would similarly imitate his teacher's work.

The puzzle was solved

with the help of

two enlightening clues

Having decided that we could identify this apprentice's work we began to note important dates on his bobbins. Returning to the censuses and records relating to Cranfield,

Fig. 16.2. From top to bottom. ➤
*"Dear Uncle", "True Love", Dear Aunt",
"Dear Mother", and a right hand spiral, wire decorated
bobbin.*

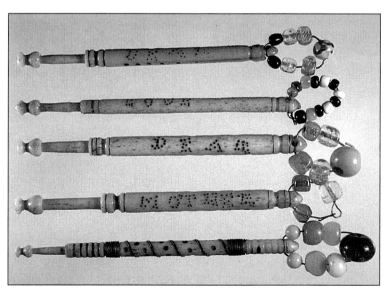

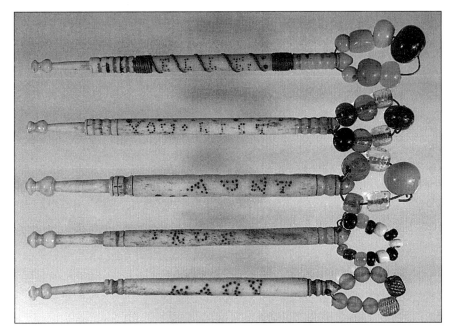

◀ Fig. 16.3. From top to bottom.
"Elle", a right hand spiral wire decoration.
"Love Don't You List" (don't join the army),
"Dear Aunt",
"True Love",
"Mary".

we searched for a person who listed himself as a bobbin maker and fitted into the time-scale we had discovered. The one son of Bobbin Brown who would have been old enough at that time had unfortunately died at Ampthill Workhouse some years earlier so we could discount him as being our mystery bobbin maker. We found only one person who would fit the bill, and this was Arthur Wright. Arthur Wright's father Samuel was a pillow maker in the village of Cranfield and would have been well known to William Brown, he may well have arranged for his son to be taken on as an "apprentice". Although Arthur was only fifteen when Brown died he would have had sufficient time to be taught the rudiments of the trade, and together with his father's trading connections with the local lacemakers he continued making bobbins for some time.

In the early years when Arthur Wright was under Brown's close supervision the quality of his work would be quite high and be sufficiently similar to his master's work to cause the confusion of identification that had initially troubled us. After Brown had died and Arthur Wright began working on his own then we feel that his standards began to fall and the difference between this young man's work and Brown's becomes more apparent. Arthur Wright's bobbins vary greatly in quality, some are almost as good as Bobbin Brown's work but others are quite poor in both choice of bone and general workmanship. Arthur perhaps

▲ Fig. 16.4.
Note the bobbin in the centre of the lace pillow made by Arthur Wright and dated 1874.

lacked the patience and attention to detail of his craftsman teacher, and it clearly shows in the bobbins he produced.

We have only discovered bone bobbins made by Arthur Wright and the majority of these were inscribed with just a Christian name or a simple romantic message such as "True Love ". It was probably lack of demand as much as lack of commitment on Arthur's part, but we have seen no bobbins dated later than the 1870's.

Samuel Wright, Pillow maker

Samuel Wright was born in Cranfield in December 1811. He was the eldest of seven children, and married Mary, a lace maker five years his senior, who died in February 1855. On Christmas Day, later that year, he married Rebecca Savage, a lace maker of "full age". Rebecca was in fact 38 when Arthur, their son was born in 1857.

It was not until the census of 1871 that Samuel describes his occupation as a lace pillow manufacturer, while a five year old granddaughter living with the family at that time is already described as a lace maker.

Thomas Wright, in his book "The Romance of the Lace Pillow", mentions Samuel Wright as a pillow maker, and his son Arthur Wright as a bobbin maker.

The 'Blunt End' Man

▲ *Fig. 17.1. A typical head and tail.*

The Blunt End Man (Working in the mid 19th century)

Again we apologise for using what might seem to be a rather flippant name for a bobbin maker, but we feel that it firstly helps describe this man's work and secondly gives him a degree of character which we feel he deserves.

This bobbin maker produced bobbins distinctly lacking the elegance or even neat finishing that characterised most of the bobbins made in the 19th century. He would saw off the end of the bobbin rather than carefully turning it as others would have done, this produced a tail end distinctly lacking in shape. It is for this reason that we have given him the nickname the "Blunt End Man". His work has little fluency, the heads of his bobbins have none of the smooth curves which we admired in the Haskins family of bobbinmakers. Sometimes the top is slightly angled, but more often it is flat. An attempt at a sweeping cut below the top is met by an angled cut from the bulb to produce the small neck. The bulb is usually flat sided and linked to the neck with a slightly angled or straight cut. The only clearly identifiable bobbins we have so far been able to attribute to this bobbin maker are made of bone with horizontal inscriptions.

Although his work might be said to lack quality and his choice of bone was poor, judging by the considerable number of his bobbins which have survived, he probably made a reasonable living. He produced a large numbers of simple inscriptions such as "Dear Aunt", "Dear Uncle", "Dear Sister", "Dear Brother", in fact he covered just about every relation a family could have in this way. These were obviously produced in reasonable numbers and formed the stock from which he sold speculatively. Others such as "Uncle Joel" or "Dear Betsy" or "Dear Samuel" would have been produced to order.

The second grouping of inscriptions is again speculative appealing to the romantic instincts of the country lacemaker, "Love Me For Ever" and "Love Me My Love". These too

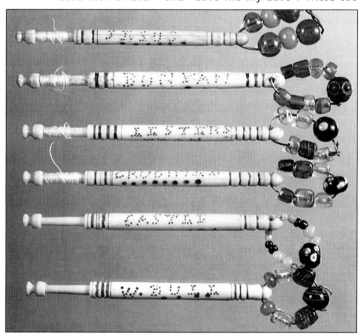

▲ *Fig. 17.3. "I Love Jesus", "John Bunyan",
"A Gift From Lesters", "William Crochtly",
"Joseph Castle Hung 1860", "W Bull Hung 1871".*

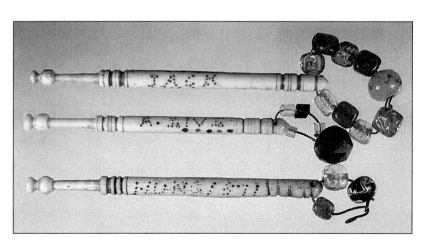

◄ *Fig. 17.2.
"Jack Alive",
"Jack A Live",
"W Bull Hung 1871."*

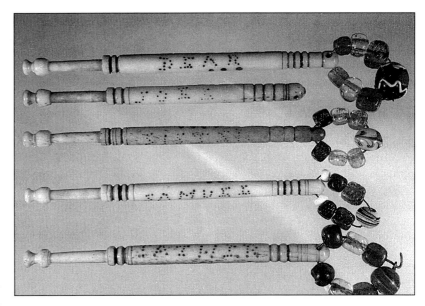

Fig. 17.4. Right, from the top. ➤
"Dear Daniel", "Dear Joel", "Dear Sister",
"Dear Samuel", "Dear Father".

probably found a ready sale amongst the young men of the lacemaking areas as they would have made appropriate gifts for their sweethearts.

A further group of bobbins is made up of religious inscriptions such as, "I Love Jesus". At first when we saw a bobbin inscribed "David" on one side and "King" on the other, we assumed it referred to a David King, but as we discovered numerous similar bobbins we realised there were simply too many for them all to refer to a David King and that it was more likely to refer to the Biblical King David. When we found further bobbins inscribed "King Solomon" and "King Pharaoh", we felt it confirmed the Biblical or religious connotations of these bobbins.

A fourth group of bobbins are those which were made to specifically order. Examples include "Rosera Right", Charles Risley", "Eliza Betts", and "William Richardson". Unfortunately we found none with a date as well as a name which might have given us a general idea of when the bobbins were made.

"Dear Aunt", "Dear Uncle",

"Dear Sister"

Most of the inscriptions made by this bobbinmaker consist of one or two lines. All can be read clearly and easily by turning the bobbin in either direction. When we came upon the inscription "Frederick - Smith My - Dear Son", on three lines, we discovered that if the head was held in the left

hand and the tail in the right, the bobbin had to be rolled in the fingers towards one's body to read the wording in the correct order. This is not the natural direction in which one would normally move the bobbin to read an inscription.

At this point it is interesting to note the square block of unturned bone which remains attached to the tail of one particular bone bobbin (see Fig. 17.8). It has not been sawn off as others have. It is a most intriguing find as it reveals quite a lot about this bobbinmaker's method of working. Firstly it shows how the square blank of bone was held in the lathe to be turned. At the headstock (the driven end at the lefthand end of the lathe) there would be a small square hole into which he pushed the squared end of the bone blank. The tailstock (at the righthand end of the lathe) would support the other end whilst the bobbin was turned. Because he turned the bobbin on the lathe with its head to his right, he must have removed it from the lathe (with the square block still attached to the tail) to add the inscription as all of his bobbins have to be held with the head on the left in order to be read. So unlike other bobbinmakers who may have carried out the inscribing process while the bobbin was still held in the lathe, he probably laid it on his work bench before drilling the dots which made up each letter. The bobbin would have been rotated as the diagonal or vertical lines of a letter were formed and then moved back to start the next letter. It seems that this bobbinmaker didn't always judge this movement very accurately which accounts for the slightly upwards slope to each line of lettering.

Besides this twist to his inscriptions, another distinguishing feature of his work can be seen in the lettering itself. The horizontal bar in many of the letters is often missed out altogether or appears to have slipped. The letter A looks like

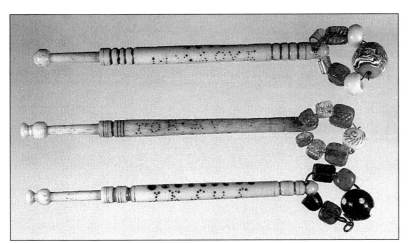

◄ *Fig. 17.5. Left, from the top.*
"Love Me My Love", "Love Me For Ever",
"I Love Jesus".

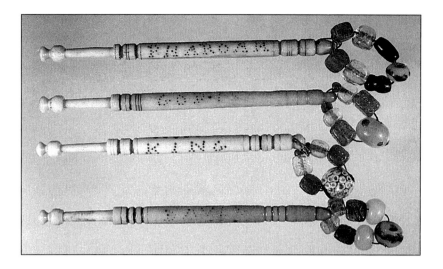

◄ Fig. 17.6. Left, from the top.
(Religious inscriptions). "King Pharoah",
"God Is Love", "King David", "King David".

▼ Fig. 17.7. Below, from the top.
"Rosera Right", " Charles Risley",
"William Richardson", "Thomas Clayson".

an upside down V. The letter H can be mistaken for an N. The E is difficult to read as the central horizontal often consists of a single dot which has slipped into contact with the lower line and the F almost always appears like the letter T.

The lettering and bands around the top and tail of the bobbin are usually coloured in black and red although an occasional bobbin can be found coloured in red only. On the opposite side of a single line inscription or, as divisions between the two lines of an inscription, he sometimes added a series of heavier dots which were drilled and coloured in the same way as the finer dots of the lettering.

In the photograph 17.8 below, there is another rather strangely inscribed bobbin. On one side it appears to have the letters SQUNT and on the other, (this is clearly seen in the photograph), the letters WLTE which have been obscured by drill dots. Was this a practice piece, or a mistake, and did he sell the bobbin, perhaps at a reduced price, or did he just give it away ?

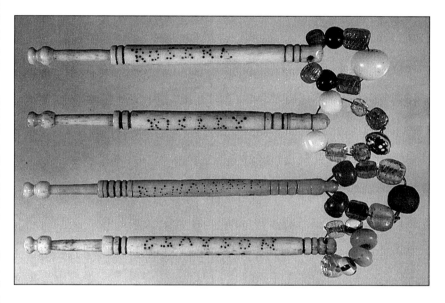

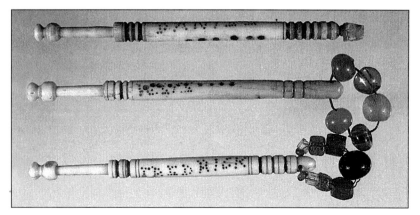

▲ Fig. 17.8. Above, from the top.
"Uncle Daniel" (this bobbin has the uncut block still on the end),
"SQUNT WLTE" (is this a practice piece?), "Fredrick" (with a real twist).

A fifth category of bobbins is made up of a group of both notable and nowadays, sought after, inscriptions.

According to Tom Huetson in his book "Lace & Bobbins", the bobbin inscribed "Jack Alive" refers to a sailor returning home safe and well. The relieved mother then commemorates the happy event on a bobbin. We have no better explanation other than to suggest that it might have been an expression or catch phrase of the time.

Bobbins inscribed "John Bunyan" commemorate the statue of the author, John Bunyan, which was erected in Bedford in 1874.

Some of the more famous inscriptions which this bobbinmaker produced are of course, hanging bobbins which are nowadays bought and sold for large sums. He inscribed bobbins "William Bull Hung 1868", and "Joseph Castle Hung 1860". Considering the rather poor quality of his bobbins , it is perhaps surprising that they sell for so much.

He would have been wealthy indeed if he had received even a small part of the price these bobbins fetch today.

One of his bobbins which we find of most interest is the one which carries the inscription "A Gift From Lesters". As this turner often failed to add the lower horizontal in the letter F, and also because his spelling was poor, the inscription which was intended to read as above unfortunately reads "A Gitt From Leters". Did he know something we didn't?

This inscribed bobbin was commissioned by the Lester family who were lace dealers in Bedford. They used the bobbin for advertising as a form of trade card, or as one tale goes, it was given to a fortunate few of his lacemakers in recognition for their good work. What we find intriguing is, why would dealers, who apparently had very high standards when it came to the work expected from their lacemakers, choose to buy bobbins from such a poor quality bobbin maker? However, it is also suggested that the lacemakers were

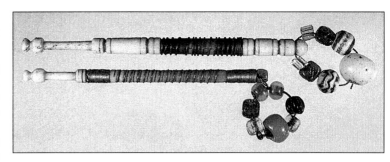

▲ *Fig. 17.9. Two less common decorated bobbins made by the "blunt end" man.*

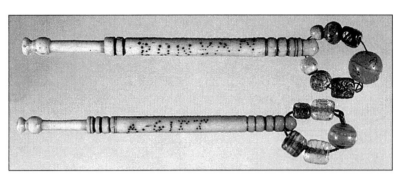

▲ *Fig. 17.10. "John Bunyan", "A Gift From Leters".*

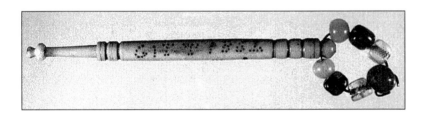

◀ *Fig. 17.11. A New Years Gift 1864."*

▼ *Fig. 17.12. The block left uncut on the end of a bobbin.*

given a plain bobbin which they then took to their local bobbinmaker to be inscribed with wording of their choice.

The hanging bobbins, the John Bunyan and the Lester bobbins all show a definite link with Bedford town or the surrounding area. They also give us some idea of the years in which he was working. We know that he was definitely making bobbins between the years of 1868 and 1874, but we have not yet been able to discover the name of a bobbin maker who might have been responsible for these bobbins. Perhaps the "Blunt End" man prefers to remain anonymous.

Archibald Abbott 1815 – 1885

Fig. 18.1, 18.2, 18.3 & 18.4. The head shape and various tail shapes which Archibald Abbott turned on his bobbins.

Archibald Abbott of Bedford is the only bobbin maker known to have stamped his name on the bobbins he made. He was a wood turner by trade, and is listed as such in the Bedford Trade Directories of 1854 and 1864, when his premises were in Cemetery Road (also known as Foster Hill Road). Even in the 1885 Directory, compiled in the year he died at the age of seventy, he is still described as a wood turner at 4, Adelaide Square.

▲ *Fig. 18.5.*
The Abbott named stamp on the bobbin tail.

Fig. 18.6. Right. Mother and babe. ➤

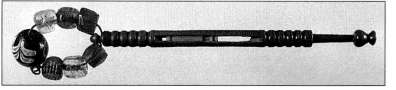

Although he was not a specialist bobbin maker his work was very well known, perhaps due to his unique practice of "signing" some of his wooden bobbins. Thomas Wright refers to him in his book as being particularly noted for his pewter Butterfly bobbins, but in fact we have seen far more Tigers of his than any other design. He also made pewter Leopards and a great number of plain wooden bobbins decorated only with a spiralling "screw thread" groove.

The "screw thread" decoration was added to many of his bobbins. Even those inlaid with pewter have this tight spiralled groove running continuously from one end of the bobbin to the other, engraving wood, bone and pewter alike. When this screwthreading does not start close to the end of the shank of a pewter inlaid tiger, it is worth looking very closely to see if any trace of the impression of his name stamp can be seen. Abbott, as a turner, probably stamped all his woodworking tools with his name, and he used a similar metal name stamp to identify some of his bobbins. We have been able to establish the existence of well over four dozen

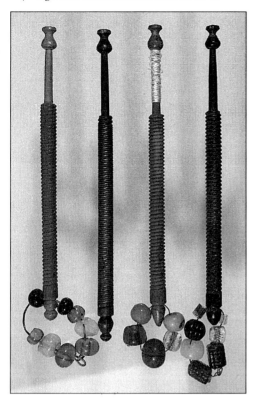

▼ *Fig. 18.7. Below. Screwthread decoration.*

onto that rotating blade cutting the first window, he then lifted the bobbin, turned it through 90 degrees, and lowered it again to cut the second window. The third and fourth windows were cut in a similar dangerous manner.

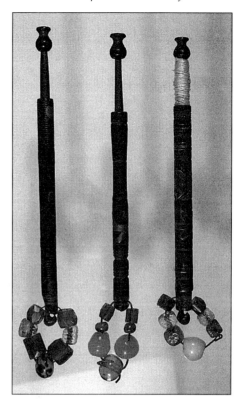

▼ *Fig. 18.8.*
Pewter leopard and two butterflies.

bobbins named in this way and every single one of them is a pewter tiger.

Besides his everyday bobbins Archibald Abbott made some more interesting examples. Less commonly seen are his mother and babe bobbins. On close inspection of this boxwood bobbin, the curve of the circular saw, which he used to cut the windows, can clearly be seen at the start and finish of that opening. It would appear that he set a 6 inch (150 mm) diameter circular saw into whatever simple machine he had, then carefully lowered the bobbin body

Abbott also inscribed bobbins both in wood, usually boxwood, and in bone. If he inscribed a single name then often on the reverse side of the bobbin he would drill out large dots and fill them with colour as a decoration. Among the more notable inscriptions which he produced are "John

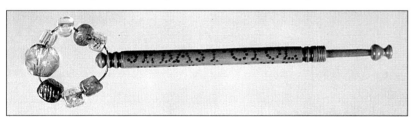

◀ *Fig. 18.9. "Sebastopol Took Sep 1855".*

Fig. 18.10. "Emma Malt", a trade bobbin. ▶

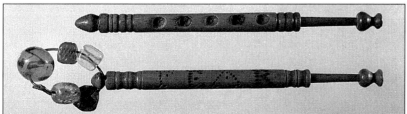

◀ *Fig. 18.11. The reverse of an inscribed bobbin and "Fear God".*

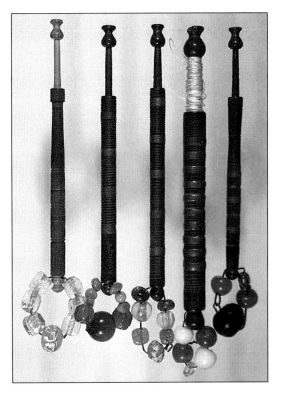

Fig. 18.12. Five pewter inlaid tigers. The second from the left is stamped "Abbott" at the tail.

The colour of many of these dyed bobbins remains so vivid today that they look as though they have just left the dye bath even though they are well over 100 years old. He employed a most interesting technique when dyeing some of his bone bobbins. First he would turn the bone into a round stick or dowel. This bone dowel would then be dyed, before returning it to the lathe to be turned into a bobbin. The areas turned away would leave the white of the bone exposed in contrast to the unturned dyed portion. To obtain these bright colours Abbott would have used the new aniline dyes, derived from coal, which gave a brilliant and permanent colour.

Identifying an Abbott bobbin is easy if it is one of the few which bears his name stamp. However, in most cases it will be necessary to look for other distinguishing feature. Abbott's bobbins had quite distinctive tail ends. The most common is almost like a separate round bead which has been added to the tail end of the shank. Sometimes he turned this bead to a more pointed shape, and occasionally he turned a rather more decorative "double bead".

The shape of his bobbin head is less unique, but is generally characterised by a rather bottom heavy, pear shaped bulb which sweeps up into a thick short neck and a flat, turned rim top. Once you have studied the head of a typical "Abbott" bobbin they become quite easy to identify.

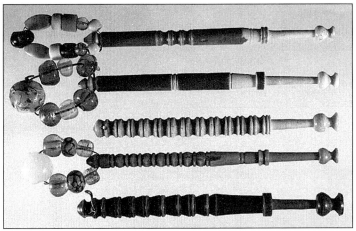

Bunyan", and "Sebastopol Took Sep. 1855". Both of these bobbins were made in Boxwood, the first commemorates the raising of the statue to John Bunyan, the second commemorates the British victory in the Crimean war. Abbott made a number of bone bobbins inscribed with the name "Emma Malt". She owned a drapers shop in Thrapston, Northamptonshire, and probably used the bobbins as "trade cards". (More details can be found in the "trade bobbin" section.)

A favourite form of decoration which Abbott used was dyeing. He dyed both wood and bone bobbins in a variety of shades from brilliant purple to veridian green.

▲ *Fig. 18.13. Dyed bone bobbins.*

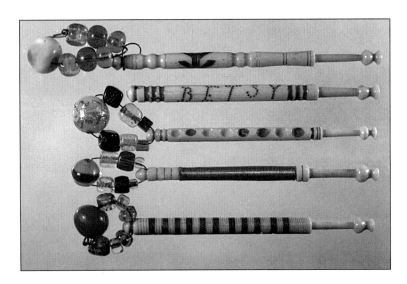

◄ *Fig. 18.14. Bone bobbins made by Archibald Abbott.*

Bobbin Maker No. 1
– No dates known

We feel that it is important to note the work of the following four bobbin makers even though we do not know their names, the years in which they were working or where they lived. Though we know so little about them they produced sufficient numbers of bobbins to allow us to learn to recognise each one's own distinctive style of work. We are sorry that, at least for the moment, they will remain anonymous.

▲ Fig. 19.1. Head and tails of
bobbin maker No. 1.

Although this bobbinmaker was probably not as prolific as some of the other makers of the 19th century, his inscribed bone bobbins really stand out. He was the only worker to have used straight lines to construct the letters of these bobbins. Occasionally those straight lines may, with the careful use of a small file, be given curved ends. Many of the letters are either completed with a drilled dot or a further straight line as a serif. The colours most commonly used on these bone bobbins are red and green or just red alone.

The head of the bobbin is well formed, the top often ending in a delicate curve. The short neck tapers from the

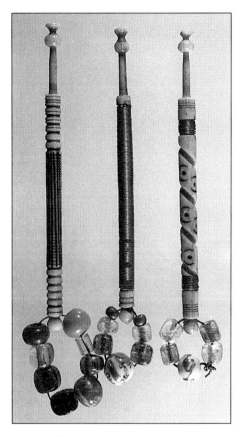

▲ Fig. 19.3. Left to right.
Crocodile, wire decoration and porthole decoration.

► Fig. 19.2. The characteristic straight letter
inscription and decoration of bobbin maker No. 1.

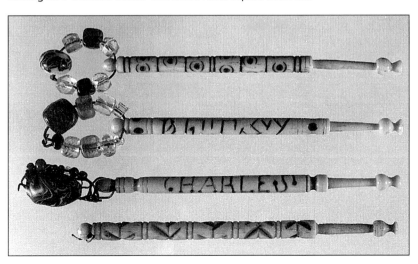

top and sweeps easily into the bulb which is usually slightly larger than the top. The bulb is well rounded, though one or two of these bobbins have flat sided bulbs. The tail ends in a small bead, which is sometimes rounded, and at other times slightly wedge shaped.

So far we have only seen bone bobbins made by this turner, but we think that these bobbins were made in the early part of the nineteenth century, so it is possible that if he made wooden bobbins they may have become so well worn that they are more difficult to identify.

He used a wide variety of decoration on his bobbins including wire binding and spiral grooves filled with tinsel for fairings. He added a series of filed V's set in opposite directions to form an arrow pattern, which was then filled with colour. He also used a most distinctive "porthole" marking in which the centre dot is coloured red and the outer circle green. However our favourite form of decoration, used by this bobbinmaker is the "crocodile". It was given this name by Mrs Fent and her daughter for it is unmistakably crocodile -like. The centre portion of the bobbin has a series of closely cut grooves with numerous parallel horizontal cuts bisecting those grooves. If this is not enough to give the impression of crocodile skin then the green colouring completes the effect.

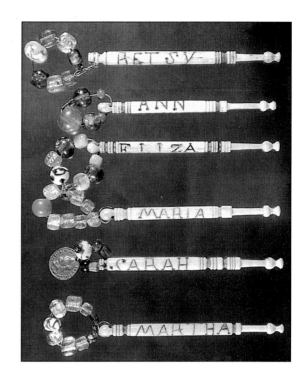

Fig. 19.4. Six bone bobbins with straight letter inscription. ➤

Bobbin Maker No. 2
– No dates known

left plain to sweep smoothly down towards the shank which is neatly turned with a mixture of ridges, beads and grooves.

Age and neglect has taken its toll on many of these bobbins. Today they often appear chipped and rather battered but when they were new they must have looked quite crisp and sharp. They have survived in considerable numbers, so this bobbinmaker must have been quite popular in his day.

◀ *Fig. 20.1. Typical head(s) and tail(s) of maker No. 2.*

▼ *Fig. 20.2. Four well used wooden bobbins which have never been spangled.*

The head, neck and collar are the most easily identifiable parts of this bobbin makers work as the body shaping varies so much from one bobbin to the next. He produced solely wooden bobbins using fruit woods which have now aged to a beautiful rich brown.

The small neck is formed where the straight cut from the top of the head meets the bulb. The bulb is well formed but squashed in shape. The squat neck tapers to the thick collar which is decorated with incised lines. Occasionally a small shape is turned beneath the collar, more often it is

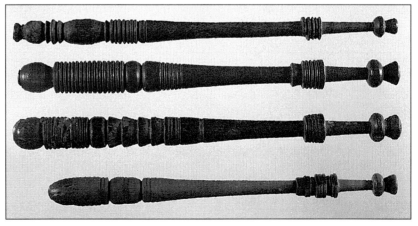

Bobbin Maker No. 3
– No known dates

Working in wood this turner's bobbins have several distinctive features. The top of the head is usually slightly angled and it rounds over to meet the line which forms the top of the small neck. The whole head is rather compressed in shape, a V cut separating the top and bulb forms the small neck.

The neck, which is thick and short, flares out and down to meet the large grooved collar. Beneath the collar the body gently widens to the main part of the shank which is decorated with a variety of turned shapes. This turner had sufficient skill and understanding to use beads, grooves, coves, incised lines and the "bees knees" shaping to produce well-balanced and well-designed bobbins. When these bobbins were made they would not have had a polish or finish applied to their surface. The beautifully smooth feel and gentle shine that most of these bobbins have today, is the result of continuous use by generations of lacemakers.

Many of these bobbins have not been drilled to take a spangle and this is not accidental. It is most likely that these bobbins were made in the early part of the nineteenth century and were intended to be used to make fine Buckinghamshire point lace. The bobbins were considered to be sufficiently heavy without needing to add a spangle of beads to their tail end.

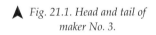

▲ *Fig. 21.1. Head and tail of maker No. 3.*

◄ *Fig. 21.2. Four nicely turned wooden bobbins.*

Fig. 21.3. Note the thick tapered necks of these bobbins. ➤

Bobbin Maker No. 4
– No known dates

Fig. 22.1. Typical heads and tails produced by maker No. 4.

▼ *Fig. 22.2. Four wooden bobbins.*

This bobbin maker, although not prolific, produced sufficient quantity to make his work worth recording. Using hawthorn and fruit woods such as plum, pear and apple, he produced workable, pleasantly turned bobbins. The head shape of these bobbins is normally well rounded with the top and bulb being of the same diameter. A slight curve over the top of the head sharply meets the line of the small neck, which smoothly sweeps into the well rounded bulb. Occasionally, the head shape may be more angular. The long neck tapers into the body and is separated from it by a collar which is often decorated with deeply cut V grooves. The main form of decoration employed by this turner is the turned bead and the deeply incised lines which are clearly seen in what can be described as "tomato sandwiches" – two flat pieces of bread and a whole tomato followed by two more pieces of bread. This "tomato sandwich" is almost always seen on some part of the bobbin made by this turner.

One indication that this work is from the early part of the nineteenth century comes in the form of the staple fixed in the tail of some of these bobbins. This staple, formed by bending a brass pin into a U shape, is pushed into pre-drilled holes in the tail and is set in position to accept the spangle wire holding the ring of beads. The top section of the pin, including the pin head, would have been cut from the pin prior to making a staple from the lower section. The top part would not have been wasted as it is often found pushed into the top of the bobbin head as an added decoration. This use of a staple to attach the spangle to the bobbin appears to have been popular only in the early years of the nineteenth century.

The Saunders Bros. of Waddesdon Late 19th & early 20th century

◄ *Fig. 23.1. Typical head and tail shapes produced by the four brothers.*

▼ *Fig. 23.3. Richard's favourite pattern, turned "beads" forming the shank of the bobbin.*

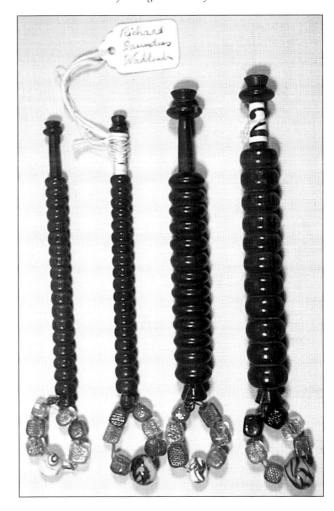

In the late 19th century and early 20th century there were four brothers in the Waddesdon area of Buckinghamshire who all made bobbins. Richard, Thomas, John and Jonah Saunders were primarily furniture makers, and this helps to explain the wide variety of woods which they used to make their bobbins. The bobbins they produced were certainly well turned, but they tend to be rather large, and somewhat lacking in style.

The head shape of the bobbin is very easily recognised. The top is slightly rounded, meeting the V wedge that abruptly joins the flattened pancake of the bulb. This V wedge forms the small neck above the bulb which is much wider in diameter than the top.

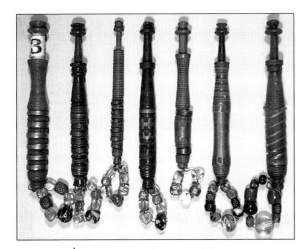

▲ *Fig. 23.2. Jonah's pewter inlay.*

Considering that these bobbins are the work of four brothers it is perhaps surprising that there is so little variation in the shape of the bobbin head. This makes it quite impossible to distinguish the work of one brother from another. However we were interested to find this passage written by Elsie Turnham (1886-1952) who lived in Waddesdon. Elsie's nieces, Di and Mary Adams, kindly allowed us to look through Elsie's collection of bobbins and attached to a set of bobbins was the following information:-

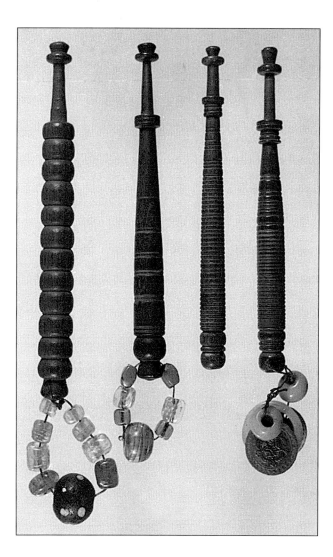

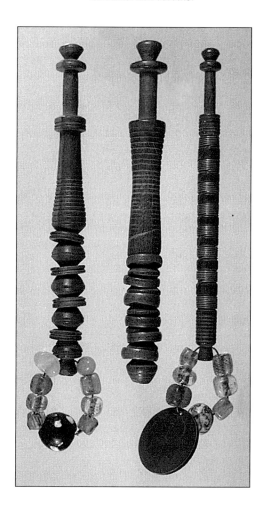

◀ Fig. 23.4. A caterpillar and three
plain turned bobbins.

▼ Fig. 23.5. Wood loose rings,
pewter loose rings and
wire decorated bobbins.

"Set of bobbins made for various Waddesdon lace makers by Richard Saunders. This is a favourite pattern of his, and it was a custom of his to say, on delivering an order [to a lace class], that he had made a gimp to match and the one who made the most lace was to have the gimp. His brother Thomas (at Quainton), John and Jonah were also bobbin makers. The last named made the lead inlay bobbins and explained to Mr John Garrick how they were done i.e. the grooves are first cut in the bobbin, and then the bobbin is carefully wrapped in brown paper. Molten lead is then poured in between the paper and the bobbin, and when cold the surplus lead is trimmed off on the lathe."

All lacemakers of Waddesdon

preferred wooden bobbins to bone

The "favourite pattern of Richard's" referred to was a simple row of turned beads down the shank of the bobbin producing a caterpillar-like appearance. The pewter inlay work which Jonah created was exceptional. He inlaid spirals and crown shapes and often undercut the pewter bands to form jingles or loose rings. He was a skilful worker with real talent.

Other styles of decoration used by these brothers include:- wooden loose rings, brass wire, bees knees, incised lines, and a form of continental style bobbin which retained the East Midland double head.

Elsie Turnham gives us a further piece of information, this time concerning the lacemakers of Waddesdon. She writes;

"All lacemakers of Waddesdon preferred wooden bobbins to bone, there are no bone bobbins in Waddesdon as wooden bobbins can be worked more quickly allowing lacemakers to make a better living."

Obviously this is the reason that the Saunders brothers worked solely in wood.

Early Twentieth Century Bobbins

Lacemaking enjoyed a significant revival in the first three decades of this century, not so much as a means of earning a living, but more as an interesting and useful pastime or hobby. Weldons produced a series of 2d magazines which examined each type of lace in turn and then gave instructions and patterns for working it. Various types of bobbin were produced at this time and were sold, very often by mail order, through lace equipment suppliers, rather than being purchased directly from the bobbin maker, as was the case in the last century.

J. Harris & Son Ltd, Cockermouth

▲ *Fig. 24.1. Derwent Mills, J Harris & son headquarters.*

Twentieth Century Bobbins (1)

J. Harris & Son Ltd., of the Derwent Mills, Cockermouth in Cumbria were suppliers of lace making equipment which was available directly from them by mail order, or through one of their five depots in London, Manchester, Birmingham, Glasgow and Liverpool.

The company of Jonathan Harris & Sons was based on an old family firm with extensive interests in the textile industry, founded in the eighteenth century. They were apparently engaged in producing linen thread throughout the nineteenth century, and this was probably the reason that when Jonathan Harris took over the mills in 1893 and established his own company, he undertook to supply all the lacemakers materials as well as the linen thread still produced in his own mills. This company went into voluntary liquidation in 1934.

The catalogue of lacemaking equipment produced by the company at some point between 1893 and 1934 can now be seen in Luton Museum. It is a fascinating little booklet with many photographs clearly showing the goods available and with prices to make a modern lacemaker's mouth water. It is interesting to note that they arranged special terms for "Mission Schools and Lace Industries". Along with a wide range of Harris lace, crochet and embroidery threads, they offered lace pillows, books, pricked patterns, pins, beads, parchment, prickers, machine lace braids, and a variety of

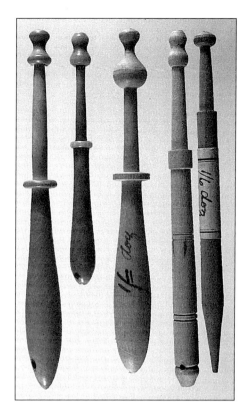

▲ *Fig. 24.2. From right to left.*
Bobbins No. 1 to No. 5. Note the price labels.

better finish than the previous two bobbins. Number 8 was made in a variety of woods, we have examples of birch, beech and box, the latter has now assumed the characteristic bent profile.

Bobbin style number 3 can be seen in the photograph (Fig. 24.5) with the words "Made In France" stamped in Ink upon its body. The bone bobbins numbered 5 and 6 are quite similar in shape to the wooden bobbins in a style more reminiscent of some continental bobbins than our own English bobbins, and may well have been made on the continent (possibly France) being imported and distributed by suppliers such as Jonathan Harris and Co. Ltd.

The bone bobbin number 7 was priced

at three shillings per dozen

Bobbin 9 is described as being made of bone, but in fact many that we have seen bear the distinctive grey smudge along one side which indicates that they were made from antler rather than bone. The shanks were decorated with identically spaced groups of ridges and hollows and had an oval tail end which was drilled for a spangle. We have seen

handmade lace edgings and insertions. They even advertised lessons in lacemaking given by a "competent and thoroughly experienced teacher" at their premises in London. A lesson lasting one and a half hours cost five shillings, and a course of six lessons cost 25 shillings. They offered both modern and old bobbins, the antique bobbins commanding surprisingly high prices compared to the modern substitutes.

The prices shown beside the bobbins in this catalogue (Fig. 24.3) have been superimposed on a previous set, but surprisingly this was not done in order to increase the prices. The new prices actually showed a very considerable reduction of up to 6d per dozen. The bone bobbin number 7 was priced at three shillings per dozen in the original printing, but as no amended price was added, it was perhaps withdrawn at this point. The original higher prices are shown in brackets on the illustration taken from the catalogue.

The company of Jonathan Harris & Sons

was based on an old family firm

The first two modern wooden bobbins illustrated in the catalogue were made of beech. The finish was rather rough, which must have been a handicap on the Honiton bobbins. The third bobbin was made in Boxwood, but because it was made out of branch wood those that survive today have frequently warped to a banana shape. These had a much

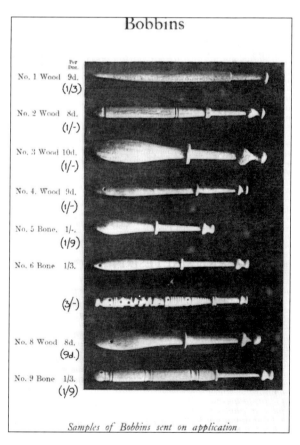

▲ *Fig. 24.3. Extract from the catalogue issued by*
Jonathan Harris & Co Ltd, between 1893 and 1934.
The previous prices of the bobbins are written in brackets.

two of these bobbins which bear additional decoration. One had coloured stripes and dots added to the shank, the other, in Luton Museum, has tiny beads in grooves cut into the two sections at each end of the shank, the centre section having been made into a compartment to accommodate a miniature "baby" bobbin.

The use of antler rather than bone for the production of these bobbins intrigued us. Having talked with a number of people who are expert in the use of bone, horn and antler we have discovered that the antlers from the Chittal and Simbar deer of India are the only ones which will provide pieces thick enough from which to turn bobbins. Could it be that these bobbins were made in India?

The heads of all the bobbins from the catalogue (with the obvious exception of the Honiton bobbin) are remarkably similar, having rather ambiguous curves and a top section which is often the same shape and proportion as the bulb. It is this feature which gives the clue for identification purposes.

The bone bobbin numbered 7 is of greater interest as the head is rather different in shape from the other bobbins and was obviously

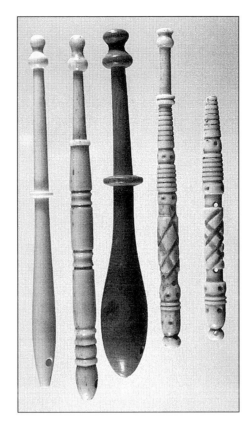

▲ Fig. 24.4. From left to right.
No. 4, No. 9 both made from antler or bone.
No. 8.
Two examples No. 7 sold undecorated.

made by a different hand. The long neck is very stout – often being fatter than the part of the shank immediately below the collar. However, it is the decoration of the shank which gives rise to most speculation, being adorned with grooves, dimples and incised lines. These are never coloured, and although the grooves on the shank have huge holes drilled, presumably to take wire, they seem to have been sold without any form of beaded, wired or tinselled decoration. We have seen many of these bobbins and in some cases have attempted to add beads and tinsel to the diagonal grooves on the shank, but these are frequently hopelessly uneven and sometimes one groove actually branches into two, so that it has proved almost impossible to achieve a satisfactory result. The maker seemed to have had no clear idea of the methods used to decorate bobbins, but added a rather random group of grooves between the two bands and left it to the purchaser to make what she could of it. This rather suggests that he might have been given an antique bobbin with spiral grooves, and told to copy it – which he did most faithfully, but with no understanding whatsoever as to the purpose of the various grooves and holes. It seems to have been quite a popular bobbin, and examples can be found without too much difficulty. Aylesbury Museum have a pair of these bobbins which the owner has attempted to complete with sealing wax rings and spots and lattice bead inlay. She purchased them at Dinton in 1905.

Despite the rather strange shaping of the heads, these seemed to be quite popular bobbins and were very much cheaper than the old bobbins offered in the same catalogue, and they survive in considerable quantities today.

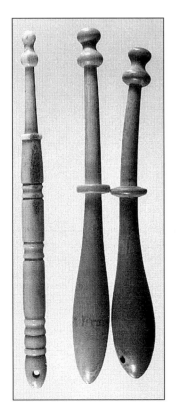

◄ Fig. 24.5.
The brown smudges clearly show on bobbin No. 9. Note "Made In France" on bobbin style No. 3, and the characteristic banana shape of the right hand bobbin.

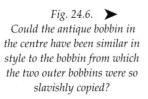

Fig. 24.6. ➤
Could the antique bobbin in the centre have been similar in style to the bobbin from which the two outer bobbins were so slavishly copied?

E. P. Rose & Son Ltd

E.P. ROSE & SON Ltd

FASHIONS · FABRICS · FURNISHINGS

48·50·52 & 54 HIGH ST. AND 2 & 4 SILVER ST. BEDFORD

TELEPHONE NUMBER 2208
TELEGRAMS ROSE. BEDFORD

▲ *Fig. 25.1. E.P. Rose billhead.*

▼ *Fig. 25.2. Bobbins sold by E.P. Rose.*

REQUISITES FOR LACE MAKING.

WOOD AND BONE BOBBINS.

		Doz.	Gross.
S12A		5¼d.	... 5/-
S12B		5¼d.	... 5/-
S12C		5½d.	... 5/-
S11		8½d.	.. 7/6
S14		11d.	... 10/6
S23		9¼d.	... 9/-
S24		11d.	... 10/6
S13		8½d.	... 7/6
S10		10¼d.	... 10/-
S21		11d.	... 10/6
S22		11d.	... 10/6
S15		1/8	... 18/-
S17		1/8	... 18/-
S18		1/10½	... 21/-
S25		5/6	... 60/-
S19		1/10½	... 21/-
S20		1/10½	... 21/-

▲ *Fig. 25.3. Extract from the catalogue by E.P. Rose & Son Ltd.*

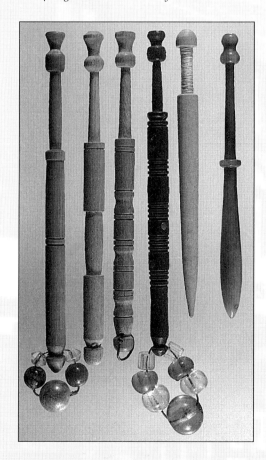

Twentieth Century Bobbins (2)

In a catalogue, very like that of Jonathan Harris and Co Ltd, E. P. Rose & Son of Bedford described a similar range of "Appliances and materials for lace making". They displayed their goods at the Ideal Home Exhibition at Olympia in 1910, so they were probably selling bobbins at the same time as Jonathan Harris, in the early years of the twentieth century.

We have seen several different catalogues distributed by E. P. Rose but even though the front cover changes, the details inside remain the same. Very few of these catalogues have survived in pristine condition, alterations to prices, "out of stock" hand written across items, and crossings out are common. E. P. Rose & Son most probably had so many

Bobbins. ANCIENT WOOD AND BONE.

Wood.	Plain **2**/- doz.	
,,	Pewter Bound **4/6** to **9/6** doz.	
Bone.	Plain and Fancy **5/6** to **9/6** doz.	
,,	With Names ... **6/6** to **12**/- ,,	
,,	With Motto, etc., **12**/- to **60**/- ,,	

Also an Assortment of Church Window Bobbins in Stock.

Fig. 25.7. Extract from the catalogue issued by E.P. Rose Ltd.

Old Bobbins

Church Window Bobbins	. . from 10/6 to 21/–	each
Bone Bobbins, with Mottoes ...	... ... 5/6	,,
Bone Bobbins, with Names, &c.	... 1/– to 3/6	,,
Various Bone Bobbins ...	... ... from 6d.	,,
Various Wooden Bobbins	... from 3d. to 6d.	,,
Pewter-bound Wooden Bobbins	... ... 6d.	,,

Fig 25.8. Extract from the catalogue issued by Jonathan Harris & Co Ltd.

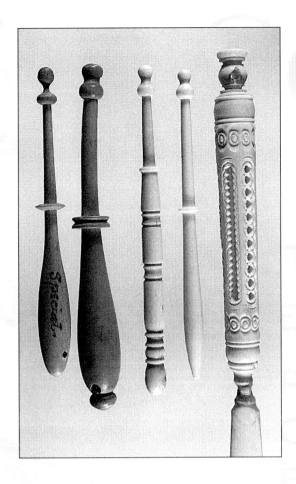

Fig. 25.4. Bobbins and decorated paperknife handle.

Fig. 25.5. Porthole decorated bobbin.

Fig. 25.6. Antique bobbins sold by E.P. Rose.

Ancient Wood and Bone Bobbins, with Antique Beads.
Name, Motto or Pewter Bound.
From **6**d. to **3/6** each.
Always a Good Selection.

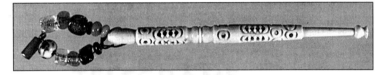

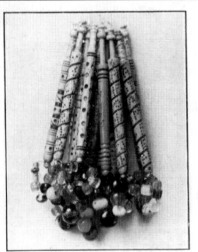

catalogues printed in one batch that, rather than re- print, the sales staff and mail order personnel were required to alter details where necessary.

There was a wide variety of both wooden and bone bobbins available, and again many look distinctly continental in origin. They sold "Ancient wooden and bone bobbins", (see illustration), which were very much more expensive than the modern bobbins illustrated in the same catalogue. They also offered to set up any lace pillow with bobbins etc. and commence the lace for "a nominal charge".

No. S25 in the illustration shows a bone (or antler) bobbin with pierced porthole decoration. In one of the photographs a similar form of decoration can more clearly be seen on the bone handle of a letter opener. When talking with Mrs May Gill of Harrogate, some years ago, she recalls several bobbins with this porthole decoration being sent to her from India where, she says, they were so abundant that the Indian children there used them for making lace. Coupled with the information about the antler being of Indian origin, could it be that these bobbins were manufactured in that country?

BEDFORD
BOLSTER
PILLOW
Fixed Bow-
front Stand as
sketch.

Set up Complete
From
21/-

They sold "Ancient wooden and
bone bobbins"

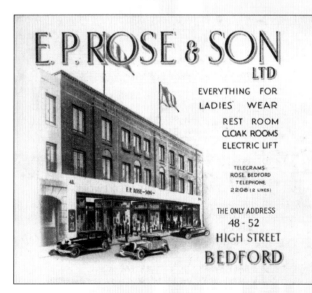

◀ *Fig. 25.9. For just over £1 a fully "set up" pillow.*

▼ *Fig. 25.10. A selection of wooden bobbins
sold by E.P. Rose.*

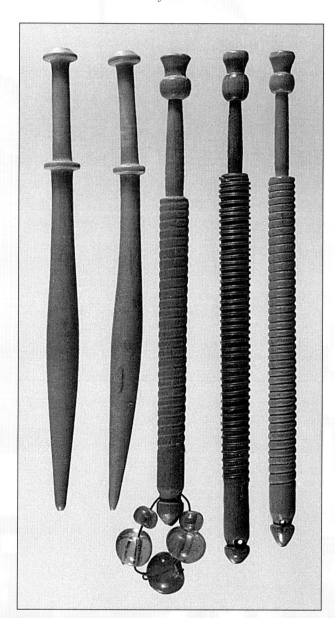

Twentieth Century Bobbins (3)

▲ *Fig. 26.1. Typical head and tail shapes.*

The most distinctive feature is the extremely uniform head with a very clearly defined "thistle" shape.

Bobbins of this style are easily identified by the shaping of the head, the lack of shaping of the "tail" and the rather heavy shaping of the shanks. They are not very elegant bobbins and have none of the interesting details of bobbins made in the previous century, but they obviously filled a gap in the market and must have been quite popular judging by the quantity in which they are in evidence today.

These bobbins were bought by the dozen from suppliers of lace equipment. They cost approximately one shilling a dozen for unspangled wooden bobbins and two shillings and four pence a dozen for bone bobbins. These particular bobbins probably date from the 1920's and 30's.

The most distinctive feature is the extremely uniform head with a very clearly defined "thistle" shape. The long neck is nicely tapered and can accommodate a good quantity of thread.

The shanks of these bobbins were turned in a wide variety of shapes. We have ten bobbins in this style, and no two are exactly alike. Some have no shaping at all on the shank, bearing just two or four incised grooves, others do have a shaped shank, which in some cases has been further embellished with ridges or grooves.

The end of each bobbin is identical, having no tail end in the way that most bobbins of the nineteenth century had. These are just rounded to a perfectly plain, blunt end which is drilled ready for spangling.

Bone bobbins of this style are particularly common today and we have seen several which previous owners have attempted to make a little more distinguished with the use of coloured dyes. We have two brilliantly scarlet bone bobbins of this era which bear no resemblance to the carmine colour achieved by bobbin makers of the last century. The result is eye-catching, but extremely garish.

The natural colouring of the wooden bobbins is not at all attractive when compared to the dark, rich shades of older wooden bobbins. They appear to have been made in a light coloured wood, (probably birch) with neither attractive colouring nor grain pattern to compensate for the plain turning.

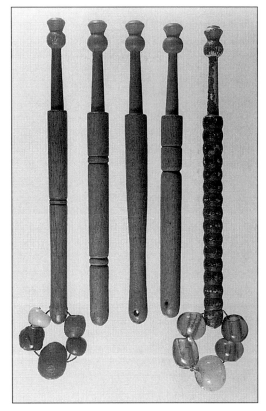

▲ *Fig. 26.2. A typical set of early twentieth century bobbins.*

Les Green, Twentieth Century

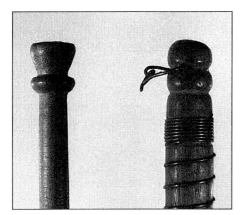

▲ *Fig. 27.1. Head and tail turned by Les Green.*

Twentieth Century Bobbins (4)

Les Green was a greengrocer in Olney, Buckinghamshire at the start of the 20th century. Although his bobbins are not particularly remarkable, it is always worth recording these details rather than allowing the information to be lost. Today his bobbins are hard to find, probably because his output was quite modest. This would have been due to the fact that he spent more time as a greengrocer than he did as a turner, and although there was a revival in lacemaking in the Olney area at the time, due to the success of Harry Armstrong's "Buckinghamshire Cottage Worker's Association", almost every lacemaker in that area had access to their mother's or grandmother's bobbins, so demand would also have been rather modest.

The shape of the bobbin head produced by Les Green is quite plain, a heavy V tapers to a flat bulb, in fact the head might well work better if it had been turned the other way up. It is quite strange, that in such a strong lace making area where advice about details such as bobbin head design would be freely given, that this head shape should be chosen or even tolerated by the lacemakers.

The only form of decoration Les added to his bobbins was wire binding. Even here Les worked in a different manner for he used copper wire rather than brass and this helps identify his work, the dull copper is so very different from the bright brass other bobbin makers used.

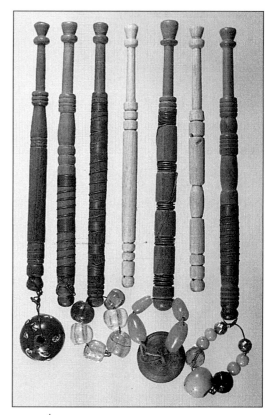

▲ *Fig. 27.2. A typical set of bobbins.*

Other known bobbin makers

The following craftsmen all made bobbins at some point during the 18th or 19th centuries, but we have not been able to find out precisely which bobbins they made.

Richard Adams of Stoke Goldington

William Johnson of Olney – listed as a bobbin maker in the "Posse Comitatus" for Buckinghamshire in 1798.

Percy Keech of Stevington – who made wooden bobbins, mainly in plum, in the 1930's.

Richard Kent of Olney – buried in Olney in 1728.

George Lumbis of Renhold

Paul Neal of Hanslop

William Pridmore of Elstow

Riseley of Elstow – who went round the villages selling his bobbins from a dog cart.

Thomas Sparke of Brayfield

Oddities

Over the years we have seen a wide variety of bobbins and there are always some which fail to fit into a set category. We have decided to gather together many of these "oddity" bobbins to show the variety of materials, methods of decoration and in some cases, the downright peculiarity of some bobbin makers. This section will deal with those bobbins.

Mother and spring?

This turned wooden bobbin has a metal spring in the central hollow rather than a baby bobbin. The use of a spring to fill this central space is not uncommon, but we have no idea why a spring should be chosen to complete the bobbin other than it being an interesting form of decoration.

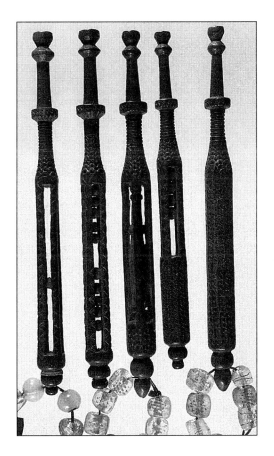

◄ Fig. 28.1. Five whittled bobbins.

◄ Fig. 28.2. Whittled bobbin.

▼ Fig. 28.3. Mother and spring, plus
three more whittled bobbins.

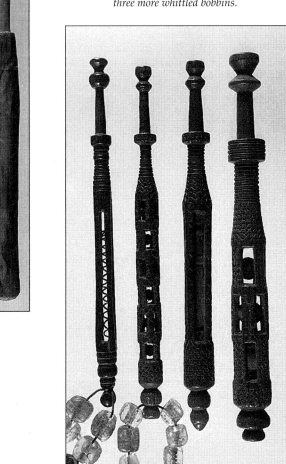

Whittled bobbins

Here you see a beautiful set of hand carved fruitwood bobbins. All the loose wooden balls and baby bobbins are carved entirely from a single piece of wood. The whole surface of the bobbin is decorated with very delicate chip carving. It is clear that these eight bobbins were made by the same highly skilled craftsman.

Two centuries ago this was the most common form of bobbin for they would have been quickly and easily made from small branches to help fill a lacemaker's pillow. They are less common now, for when lacemakers could afford better bobbins they would have discarded these in preference for a nicely turned wood or bone bobbin.

Pewter "Trolley" bobbins

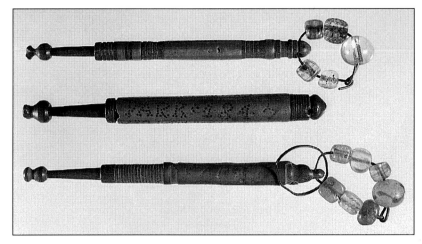

On these wooden bobbins you will see that there is a large central area covered with pewter inlay. Very often this metal area has words inscribed upon its surface in a manner similar to bone and wooden inscribed bobbins. Pewter is quite a soft material and the inscription is often well worn as can be seen on the examples in the photograph. The top bobbin's inscription is unclear. The middle bobbin reads "Kis Me If You Will My Love And Kis Me In The Park 1847". The lower bobbin with a well worn ring attached to the spangle is inscribed "Fanny Goodman My Mother."

▲ Fig. 28.4.
Pewter "Trolley" bobbins.

Pewter bobbins

This type of bobbin was, at one time, far more common than it is today. They are turned from solid pewter, and no doubt because of their weight and possibly because they bend easily, many have been discarded. The mother and babe pewter bobbin shown in the photograph has a plaque attached to its spangle, it reads "Melville Free Church Aberdeen 1867", the inscription on the reverse is indistinct.

Fig. 28.5. ➤
Pewter bobbins.

Bobbins with beads forming the shank

Examples of this style of bobbin sometimes appear to be a repair made from two dissimilar parts, yet other examples look as though the bobbin was carefully designed by the bobbin maker. The bone pewter example is made by Jesse Compton and the wooden bobbin by "the Bitted man". Many of the bobbins which have been made in this way have not survived for the beads in the centre are often held on an iron or steel pin. If this central metal spindle becomes damp it will corrode and expand bursting the glass beads or breaking the joint in the bobbin body. The bobbin in the photograph Fig. 12.16 (in Northampton Museum's collection) with only one bead remaining on the central spindle is a typical example.

▼ Fig. 28.6.
Two beaded shank bobbins.

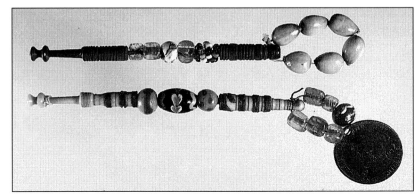

▼ *Fig. 28.7. Brass bobbins.*

Fig. 28.8. Brass mother and babe with twisted bars.

▼

Silver bobbins

Occasionally one may find a bobbin made from silver and if they are hallmarked, as they should be, then they will be easy to date. The one shown in the photograph has the name "Marie" fluently inscribed upon its surface. It was made in Chester in 1909 by SB&SI.

▲

Fig. 28.9. A silver bobbin.

Bitted

This bobbin is a real treat. The bobbin maker has been extremely clever with his use of wood inlay. Although he may not be the neatest worker he has produced an amusing group of windmills set around the bobbin.

▲

Fig. 28.10. Bitted Windmill.

Brass bobbins

Brass bobbins can be heavy and awkward to use. These bobbins may have been made for their novelty value, as an unusual gift rather than as a practical working tool. Finer, lighter examples may have been used as gimp bobbins.

The bobbin on the left with the thimble spangle is inscribed "John Wesley", the middle bobbin is a most unusual mother and babe style with the central cage made from fine beads threaded upon thin rods and the bobbin on the right is simply turned.

The mother and babe bobbin shown in photograph Fig. 28.8 is made entirely from brass. It is interesting to see the way in which the bars of the cage have been twisted to produce a delightful decorative effect. This bobbin can also be seen on Plate 21 of Thomas Wright's "Romance of the Lace Pillow".

Buckinghamshire County Museum has a fine collection of brass bobbins. Some are turned, and some are inscribed. Four of the inscriptions from those bobbins are listed below and are typical of inscriptions found on East Midland bobbins.

"My Mary 1817", "I Love The Boys", "I Will", "I Love U".

Cow and calf

This is a rare and unusual bobbin which is generally made of different coloured woods. The tail pulls out from the body to expose a baby bobbin attached to that tail.

Fig. 28.11 Cow and Calf (Right – Open). ➤

Fig. 28.12. Cow and Calf (Far Right – Closed). ➤

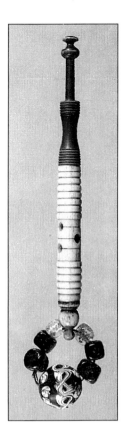

Fig. 28.13 & 28.14. Jack In The Box ◀ ▶

Tunbridge mosaic

Unfortunately we cannot show a photograph of a bobbin inlaid with a Tunbridge mosaic pattern, but we know that one exists for we were shown a very rare example by a lady in Scotland. The body of the bobbin was made up of small, naturally coloured squares of wood to form a geometric pattern. The squares were about 1.5mm (1/16 inch) in size.

Glass

It is very difficult to date glass bobbins but the one shown in the photograph probably dates from the nineteenth century. It has an opaque white top and an exquisitely twisted purple body with an opaque white ring at the tail to take the spangle. No doubt more glass bobbins were made in the nineteenth century, but few have survived.

Inscribed bone bobbin

We often come upon well made bobbins such as you see in the accompanying photograph, but they have been made in such small numbers that the makers will remain anonymous. This beautifully inscribed bobbin is just too nice to leave in obscurity, it reads "Henry Wall Pereira".

Jack in the box

The bobbin shown in the photograph is made from wood and bone. The wooden head, neck and top of the body screws into the bone shank. When the two parts are separated the baby bobbin held inside can fall or "jump" out.

Revival bobbins

During the early part of the 20th century there was a revival in lacemaking and some bobbins were made during that time perhaps by relatives of these new lacemakers. The three shown here are typical examples from that time. They are rather crudely inscribed and read from the top, "Uncle Johnie Died May 23 1912", "Eva", and "Princess Mary Married Feb. 28 1922".

▼ *Fig. 28.15. Glass bobbin.*

▼ *Fig. 28.16. A beautifully inscribed bobbin.*

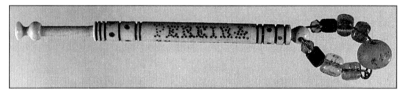

▼ *Fig. 28.17. Revival bobbins.*

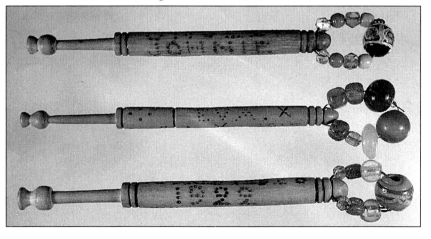

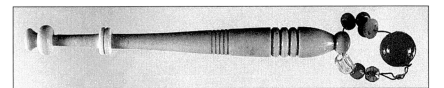

◄ *Fig. 28.18. Ivory bobbin.*

▼ *Fig. 28.19 & 28.20.* ▼
Two-headed bobbins.

Ivory bobbins

Although many antique dealers may like their customers to think that they are selling ivory bobbins, it is most unlikely because ivory bobbins are very few and far between. In our research we have only seen two ivory bobbins, both of which were made in the early 20th century. One is shown here.

Jet

This pair of South Bucks bobbins are turned from Whitby jet, very plain, very smooth and very black.

Two headed bobbins

These are a real oddity, but we have seen them in sufficient numbers for us to realise that they were made for a specific purpose, perhaps for making metal lace. The metal thread is wound on the top neck and cotton, linen or silk thread is wound on the lower neck. The two threads are worked together, the metal thread being supported and strengthened by the natural thread.

We have also been shown a more unusual antique bobbin which has a head and neck at each end, to confuse matters a spangle has been added to one (head?) end. We do not know whether the bobbin had a purpose or if it were just a bobbin maker's joke.

Cottier Bobbins

These boxwood bobbins were made in France in large numbers. These ingenious bobbins unscrew at the end to reveal a hollow chamber. A commercially wound spool is slipped inside, keeping the thread perfectly clean. The end of the thread is passed up through a small hole to the neck, the thread then passes beneath a plastic collar to the head where a hitch holds it in place. The bobbin can then be used in the normal manner.

Yak Bobbins

Yak bobbins were used to make a woollen lace. Because of the thickness of the thread the bobbins needed to be bigger and heavier than normal bobbins. This immense example is from the Northampton Museum collection.

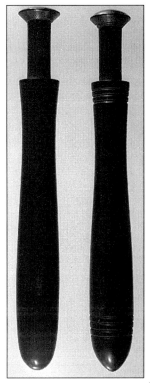

▲ *Fig. 28.21.*
A pair of Jet bobbins.

Fig. 28.22. ►
Cottier bobbin,
open and closed.

Fig. 28.23.
Yak bobbin with a
normal size bobbin
alongside for scale.
(Courtesy Northampton
Museum and Art
Gallery.)
▼

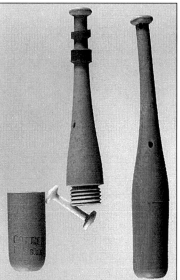

York bobbins

These large ebony bobbins are extremely heavy. The end unscrews and the hollow is filled with lead to add weight. We were told that these bobbins were used to make gold lace for the clergy at York Minister but it is also possible that they were in fact intended for weaving tapestries rather than making lace.

▼ *Fig. 28.24. York bobbins.*

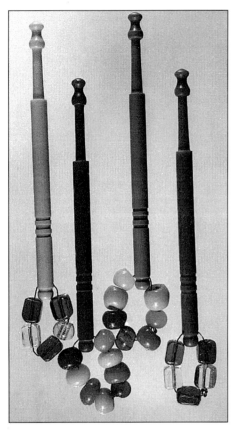

▲ *Fig. 28.25. Plastic bobbins.*

Plastic bobbins

When, in the early part of the 20th century, plastic itself was considered an oddity some turners managed to acquire pieces of this new material and made one or two bobbins as a novelty. In the photograph you will see four plastic bobbins one is bright yellow, one blue, one maroon and one green. Thousands of plastic bobbins have been produced in the last fifteen years, but these have been made by the injection moulding technique. They all have what looks like a seam on two sides of the whole bobbin whereas the early turned plastic bobbins do not have this seam.

Modern oddities

We cannot resist including this pair of bobbins, for they show, that even today, oddities are produced. In fact, with the large number of bobbin makers all trying out new methods and ideas the number of "oddities" must be increasing daily.

These two bobbins were made by Beth Schoenburg when she was living in North Jersey, U.S.A. They were made for her "pun" pillow and are a pair of SPRING—ETT bobbins.

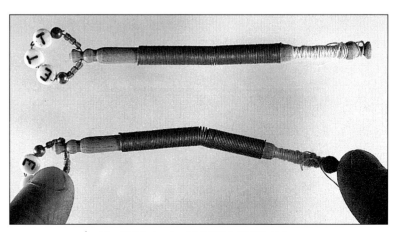

▲ *Fig. 28.26. A pair of SPRING—ETT bobbins.*

Lace bobbins from other parts of Britain

Although the study of South Bucks, Devon, Downton and Malmesbury bobbins is a specialist area in itself, we felt it would be helpful to note some details of these English lace bobbins.

South Bucks bobbins

These rather heavy looking bobbins were used to make fine Buckinghamshire point lace and are still used by some lacemakers today. The shape of these unspangled bobbins is closer to those used on the continent than those used in neighbouring counties. Although these bobbins can be found in a variety of lengths and diameters the majority are close to 90 mm (3 1/2 inch) in length and 15 mm (5/8 inch) diameter.

Bobbinmakers producing this style of bobbin were very skilful in developing a variety of decorative elements. Bobbins called "plum puddings" have light or dark wooden spots scattered over their surface. "Jingles" have loose wooden or pewter rings. The South Bucks mother and babe bobbins are often hand carved with exquisite chip carved decoration. A" Jack in the Box" contains a surprise, pull off the top or tail and a baby bobbin slides out from inside. So always take a second look at a South Bucks bobbin made from two or more woods for it may contain a secret. A gentle shake will reveal the presence of a hidden miniature bobbin.

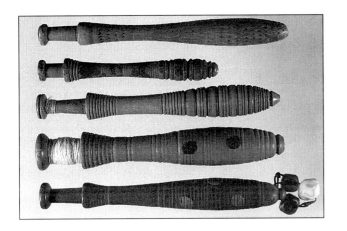

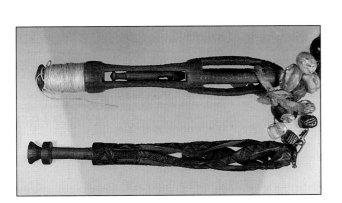

◄ *Fig. 29.1, 29.2 & 29.3 From top down.*
– Plain and plum pudding south Bucks bobbins.
– Pewter and wood jingle and "tigers".
– Carved mother and babe south Bucks bobbins.

▼ *Fig. 29.4. Jack in the box, open and closed.*

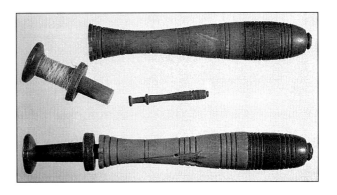

Devon bobbins

Devon bobbins are about 90 mm (3 3/4 inch) long and 6 mm (1/4 inch) diameter. The majority are usually quite plain and are made from a light coloured, dense wood such as Boxwood, Wild Service or Spindle, although some, and they are less common, were made from darker woods. One such bobbin that we have seen was made from ebony, it was incised with lettering, motifs and a date, all of which were filled with scarlet sealing wax producing the most startling effect. This particular bobbin dated from the early eighteenth century.

The more common form of inscribed Devon bobbin has symbols, dates and inscriptions incised upon its surface, in a manner similar to scrimshaw. These incised marks were filled with coloured sealing wax. Red, black, blue and sometimes green wax would have been used and the surplus rubbed or turned away leaving the bobbin body beautifully smooth. Many of the husbands of these lacemakers relied on the sea for their living, symbols such as anchors, fish, and sailing ships are commonly found upon these bobbins. Other symbols such as plants, stars, hearts, birds and the tree of life, are also used and bear a remarkable similarity to the symbols found on hand stitched samplers and Hollie point lace produced in the same period.

Aqua Fortis (Nitric acid) was used to decorate some of these bobbins

---

A simpler form of decoration called "Branscombe riggled" relied upon a series of grooves which are turned into the bobbin surface and then filled with coloured sealing wax. When the wax was dry the whole bobbin surface is rubbed smooth.

Aqua Fortis (Nitric acid) was used to decorate some of these bobbins. It was applied in trickles and wavy lines which twisted and turned all over the bobbin body. After a very short time the acid would have darkened the areas it had touched, the acid was then washed off leaving a strange mottled pattern upon the bobbin surface as the bobbin dried.

Chip carving is one other form of decoration used on the surface of Devon bobbins in the late nineteenth century. Small cuts are made to produce an open pattern. This is often more effective on items considerably larger than the relatively small surface of a bobbin.

Fig. 29.5 to 29.10. ➤
A selection of bobbins described in the text.

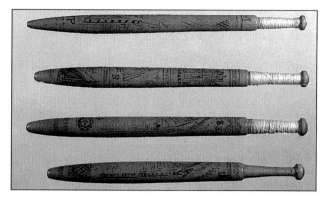

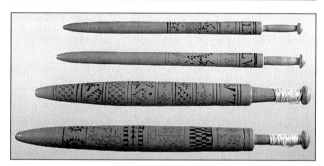

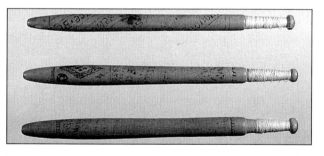
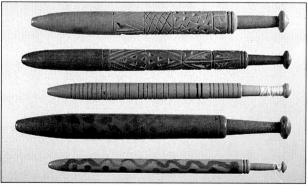

Downton bobbins

In Downton, Wiltshire, the lacemakers produced a point lace. It is interesting to note the regional variations in this type of lace and also the varied types of bobbins used to make it.

The typical Downton bobbin is short and compact, approximately 80 mm (3 1/4 inch) long and 9 mm (3/8 inch) diameter at its widest point. These bobbins are somewhat similar to the Devon bobbins, again being made from dense, light coloured woods, with a single head and pointed tail. The body itself is squat, coffin shaped and occasionally decorated in a similar manner to the Devon bobbins, although to find one with wax filled decoration in good condition is a rarity. The majority of these bobbins are quite plain or have the mottled, aqua fortis pattern on their surface.

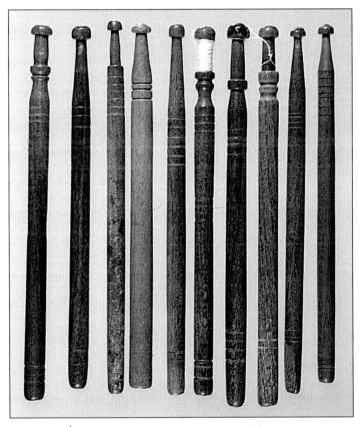

▲ *Fig. 29.12. A set of Malmesbury bobbins.*

▼ *Fig. 29.13. A bamboo bobbin from Ipswich, Massachusetts, and a smaller Malmesbury bobbin.*
A more striking resemblance can be seen with bobbins No. 2, 4, 5, 9 & 10 in Fig. 29.12.

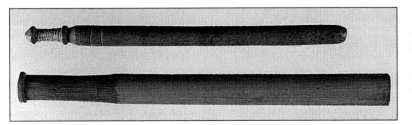

▼ *Fig. 29.11. Downton bobbins.*

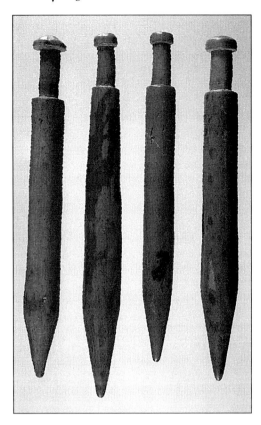

Malmesbury bobbins

These extremely plain unspangled bobbins, sometimes called Malmesbury sticks, were used to make Malmesbury lace (again a form of Point lace), in the town of that same name in Wiltshire. Turned from fruitwood or similar close grained wood, they have a domed single head and short tapered neck upon which to wind thread. The only form of decoration, if any at all, is a slight turned collar beneath the neck. Occasionally the neck tapers from the head straight into the body. These bobbins are about 100 mm (4 inch) long and 4 mm (3/16 inch) diameter.

Whilst visiting Ipswich in Massachusetts, U.S.A. we were introduced to Ipswich lace which appeared to have much in common with Malmesbury lace. Ipswich lace was made in the 18th century and was also a form of Point lace. The bobbins used to make Ipswich lace were made from bamboo and were slightly larger than those from Malmesbury but when compared (see photograph) the similarity is striking. We have found no definite links between these two lace communities but the coincidences are remarkable and worthy of further investigation.

Materials used in the making of bobbins

Ivory or Bone?

There can be few lacemakers or bobbin collectors today who have not, at some time, been invited to buy highly priced lace bobbins "which are made out of ivory". However, on closer inspection, such bobbins inevitably turn out to be made of bone. In the same way that there were a few silver bobbins and one or two extremely ornate bobbins with a japanned lacquer finish, perhaps a few were made in ivory for the Ladies of Quality, who made lace as a pastime rather than a means of earning a living. Some bobbins made more recently in India are definitely made in ivory, and contemporary bobbin makers may certainly have used this material until quite recently, but the average bobbin maker in the last century, working in a tiny cottage workshop in the depths of Northamptonshire or Bedfordshire, would commonly have had no access to such a rare and costly material and would most certainly have used bone not ivory.

Ivory is formed in a different way from bone, which gives it a distinctive "grain" pattern. This is most easily seen when a cut is made across its length, when it appears as a crisscross pattern, reminiscent of the "end grain" of wood. Marine ivory (walrus tusk, narwhal horn, whale teeth etc.) does not have this distinctive patterning, so its absence cannot always be taken as proof that the item is made of bone. It is a complex field unlikely to trouble the collector of antique bobbins. Colour cannot be considered a very good guide for identifying either material because the ivory from an African elephant can be quite different from that of a walrus or whale. Bone may vary in just the same way according to its treatment and origin.

Decorated English bobbins, genuinely made in ivory during the last century are rare, so unless a pattern of grain can be clearly distinguished, it is much wiser and probably more accurate to assume that they are made of bone.

What bone?

It is hard to know whether early historical reference to "bone lace" refers to the material used to make the bobbins or the fish bones which were said to have been used as a cheaper alternative to metal pins. However, bobbins have been made from bone for several hundreds of years, but it is hard to be sure which animals provided that bone. Bone was one of the earliest materials to be used for bobbins. According to the stories handed down from the lacemakers of the last century all sorts of bone was used.

One of the best known traditions must be that a bobbin to commemorate a wedding was made from the bone in the ham joint served at the wedding feast. However we have found that the bones from pigs of today have nowhere near sufficient thickness to make such a bobbin. This at first throws doubt on the accuracy of such a tale, but it must be remembered that the beasts which are carefully bred today to provide lean meat with the minimum of fat and bone, are very different from their ancestors of one hundred years ago. Animals then were fatter and larger boned, and they were also butchered at their point of maximum growth, rather than when they were younger, more tender and rather smaller, as is the practice today. One other answer to the supposed use of a ham bone might be that the bobbin maker on receiving the rather poor quality bone, not wanting to upset the new bride, would accept the order for the commemorative bobbin, then when the young girl had left he would place the useless piece of bone beneath his bench and choose a more suitable piece from his regular stock to make the commemorative, confident that no one would be the wiser.

Apart from having a different conformation and enjoying a rather longer life before slaughter, there was also a very different pattern of animal husbandry. One lacemaker, with a long history of lacemaking in her family told us that in her

▲ *Fig. 30.1. Left to right. Beef, Lamb and Pork bones.*

mother's village, everyone kept a pig which could be fed on scraps. These animals provided the bulk of the meat eaten in the village. Mutton or beef very rarely appeared on their dinner tables.

Today there are few bones which provide any great thickness for the bobbin maker. The most satisfactory is the shin bone from the back leg of a beef animal, but rarely does it yield such immense thicknesses enjoyed by the craftsmen of the last century, when bone bobbins of amazingly generous proportions appear to have been quite commonplace.

▼ *Fig. 30.2 . The telltale flecks characteristic of bone are particularly noticeable on the neck of the bobbin shown below.*   *Fig. 30.3. Note the grey "smudge" mark of antler.* ▶

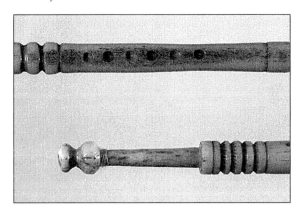

Mutton bones, also frequently mentioned as a source of bone for bobbins, today are so thin in cross section that it makes it rather hard to believe that they ever provided a useful source of bone for the bobbin maker.

There were two animals which were extremely commonplace at the time when bone bobbins were being made, and which could have provided bones of considerable thickness. It seems reasonable to assume that the bones of the extremely powerful working horses and oxen would be both large and heavy, but unfortunately such bone would be very difficult to acquire today in order to put this theory to test.

Decorated English bobbins,

genuinely made in ivory during

the last century are rare

So where would bobbin makers obtain their bone? During the 18th and 19th centuries an enormous number of tallow candles were made and used. To produce tallow, bones, fat and other parts of animal carcasses are boiled down. The fat which floats to the surface is then refined into tallow for candle making and lubricants. The clean bone which remains would be sold to a bone merchant who would use it to make fertiliser or sell as a material for craftsmen.

The bobbin maker might buy bone from a tallow chandler or a bone merchant, choosing those pieces which he considered thick enough. He would not know whether the bone was ox, beef or shire horse, just that it was good enough for bobbin making.

Antler

The largest number of bobbins made from this material were produced at the start of the twentieth century. A great number of these were supplied by the Cockermouth firm of Jonathan Harris. These bobbins feel rather heavier than a bone bobbin of similar size and may have a very distinct grey "smudge" down one side where some of the outer surface colour has been included. Most antlers have very thin walls containing insufficient material from which to turn a bobbin. Two species however, do produce antlers with a very thick wall and these are the Simbar and Chittal deer from India.

Woods

Most lace bobbins were made from wood. It was cheaper, more plentiful and both quicker and easier to prepare than bone. It did not lend itself to quite such elaborate or colourful decoration, but it enabled a bobbin maker to produce simple, cheap bobbins in large quantities, which found a ready sale.

As with bone, the bobbin makers used whatever woods were locally available. With so many fruit trees in every garden it is not surprising that fruit woods were widely used. Apple, pear, cherry and plum all give good close grained timber ideal for small turned items such as bobbins. The rich dark colour of some varieties of plum made it especially attractive, and it was perhaps the most widely used of the fruit woods, apple, pear and cherry being much paler in comparison. The 19th century bobbin maker would have used whatever wood came his way. A hawthorn trunk blown down from a hedgerow or even a substantial branch from a walnut tree brought down in a gale would have been gratefully accepted. When the pit sawyer, an itinerant workman, next arrived in the village, those carefully collected trunks and sizeable branches would be taken to the saw pit to be cut into useful size planks. The planks would then be stacked in the bobbin maker's yard with small sticks separating them, allowing air to blow through slowly drying the wood over several seasons – hence the name seasoning.

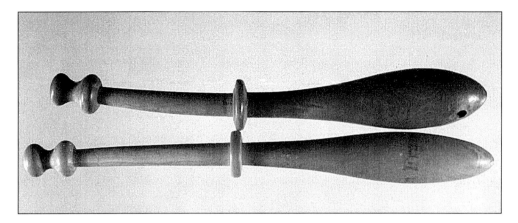

◀ Fig. 30.4.
Banana shaped
Boxwood bobbins.
The bobbins have warped
because branch wood was used
rather than the more stable
wood from the trunk.

Boxwood is one of the hardest and most closely grained of our home grown timbers and it was widely used by bobbin makers during the 19th century and in the early years of the 20th. The nineteenth century maker used his boxwood very sparingly, inserting small strips into elaborate patterns of grooves to make "bitted" bobbins. The close grained nature of the boxwood inserts allowed the bobbin to be worked without the bits picking up the darker colouring of the main part of the bobbin.

At the beginning of the twentieth century new lace bobbins were mass produced rather crudely in beech or birch. Some rather better quality bobbins were made in boxwood in a shape rather reminiscent of the more bulbous continental bobbins. Again the Cockermouth firm of J. Harris sold large quantities of these bobbins. Unfortunately many seem to have been made of branch wood, rather than the more stable wood of the trunk, with the result that over the years, the bobbins have warped and assumed a very banana-shaped profile.

All the common hedgerow and woodland trees yielded material for the bobbin maker, but it is often quite difficult to identify the wood of old bobbins as most tend to take on a rather uniform dark brown colour, and in such small pieces the grain is often too indistinct to allow for positive identification without detailed analysis.

Dyeing bobbins

Both wooden and bone bobbins were coloured by immersion in various dyestuffs. The colours used did not penetrate the bone very deeply, and on the most prominent surfaces of the bobbin, the colour has frequently worn away, or in some cases was deliberately turned away when it was made, leaving the colour in protected channels and grooves.

Most of the dyes have faded with prolonged exposure to daylight, this is true of antique green bobbins in particular. However, the neck has been protected from the light by the thread wound round it, so it is this area of the bobbin which is most likely to retain its original colouring, which may be startlingly different from the colour on the rest of the bobbin.

Both natural and chemical dyestuffs were used to colour bobbins. A very deep, reddish purple dye was obtained by boiling chippings from the Central American logwood tree in water. This produces a very strong dye, capable of dyeing bone to a very dark shade. This material would have been readily available to bobbin makers of the nineteenth century.

---

it is perhaps best known for producing the

distinctive red coat of the British soldier

There are two possible natural sources of dye used to produce the shade of carmine so frequently found on old bone bobbins. The vividness of the colour suggests that it might be a dye of chemical origin, but in fact it is most likely to have been derived from cochineal (the dried and powdered remains of an insect which lives on cactus in Mexico). This dye was well known for many years before it was used for dyeing bobbins, and it is perhaps best known for producing the distinctive red coat of the British soldier in previous centuries. (Stannous chloride being used as a mordant to produce a redder shade of scarlet).

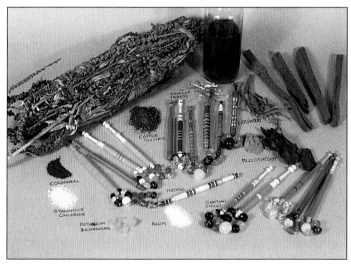

▲ *Fig. 30.5. Above. Bobbins and dyestuffs.*

Cudbear (a dried and powdered lichen) is the second possible source of red dye, but unfortunately we have not been able to obtain any with which to carry out our own experiments.

Several chemical dyes were also used. The bright veridian green of many antique bobbins is thought to have been obtained from arsenate of copper, but as this is a poisonous substance, which requires careful handling, we have not attempted to ascertain the truth of this statement. We have tried to achieve this vivid shade of green with a large variety of natural dyestuffs, but all gave a very much yellower green than the malachite green revealed under the thread on the neck of an old bobbin. This tended to confirm the view that the dye is chemical in origin.

There are a small number of very highly coloured bone bobbins which were most probably made at a later date than bobbins dyed with the previously mentioned substances. A particularly vivid shade of yellow was achieved using potassium bichromate, and a strong, rather lurid shade of mauve, was produced using gentian violet (a combination of methyl rosaline, methyl violet and crystal violet). The bobbins then had some parts re-turned to give startlingly white bands as decoration on the shank. Some wooden bobbins also show traces of having been dyed with gentian violet. Archibald Abbott dyed many of his bobbins using the "new" aniline dyes which are coal derivatives. These colours were brilliant at the time of dyeing and have remained so over the years.

Coloured Dots & Grooves

Only the simplest colouring of grooves and dots was possible on wooden bobbins. Red and blue were mainly used to pick out dots of the letters of names, or very short inscriptions. A wider variety of colours could be used on bone bobbins including red, blue, black, yellow and green. These colours were produced by mixing powdered paint with gum Arabic, and then painting it into the grooves or dots with a brush or quill. Any surplus was easily wiped off the surface of the bobbin.

This type of colouring is soluble in water, and that is why bobbins which have been stored in damp conditions often lose their colour. It also tends to wear off very easily where the grooves, slashes or spots are not of sufficient depth to protect the paint.

Pewter inlay

Many bobbins, both bone and wooden, were decorated with a metal inlay. A pattern of grooves and channels was made in the shank of the partly completed bobbin, and then molten metal was poured in. The metal inlays of bobbins decorated in this way, can take on an exceedingly attractive shine when frequently used. This has led many people to believe that because the metal shines like silver, that it is indeed inlaid with silver, but this is not true. The metal is in fact pewter, an alloy of tin and lead.

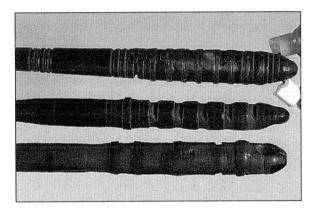

▲ *Fig. 30.7. "Flash" marks and "key" cut.*

Different bobbin makers used pewters composed of quite different proportions of tin, lead and antimony (an additive which gave improved lustre), but on average pewter has a melting point of 225°C which allows it to be poured into a wooden bobbin without even scorching the wood. Silver has a melting point of 960°C, which could never be poured into a wooden bobbin because wood will spontaneously ignite at a temperature of only 275°C. Although we have not been able to put it to the test we feel that it is equally unlikely to be successful on a bone bobbin.

this was a technique frequently used by the old bobbin makers

▲ *Fig. 30.6. Pewter tankards, a bobbin makers source of pewter?*

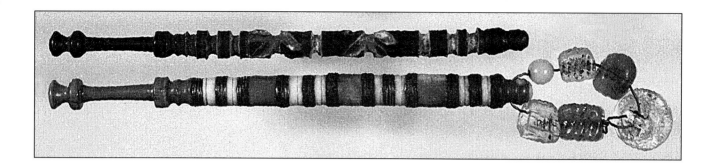

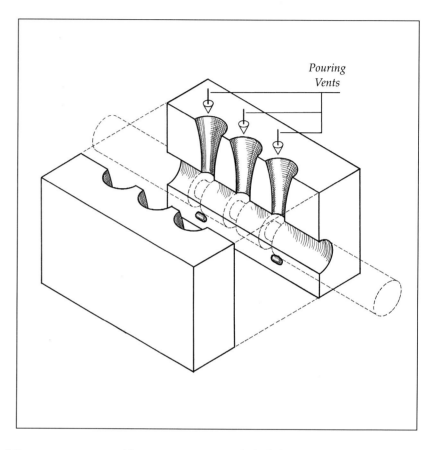

▲ *Fig. 30.8. One good and one poor pewter inlaid bobbin made by Jesse Compton. The one with no remaining pewter is made of wood, the other of bone to which bistre coloured dye has been applied in some areas.*

Fig. 30.9. A simple mould for casting ▶
pewter into bobbins.

Pouring Vents

The intricate pattern of inlay achieved by some makers, and the presence of a line of "flash" on one side of some bobbins could not have been produced if silver or pewter sheet had been cut to shape and merely applied in a shallow groove. Anyone who has ever tried to replace the missing pewter inlay of a "butterfly" bobbin using pewter foil, will surely agree with this view.

When we first attempted to discover how pewter inlaid bobbins were made, we soon found that a ring of pewter (as on a "tiger") would very easily work loose and would twist round, free of the bobbin. To prevent this, we found that a "key" in the form of an angled saw cut at the bottom of the groove, prevented the ring from becoming loose with use. Examination of many antique bobbins which have lost their pewter, clearly shows that this was a technique frequently used by the old bobbin makers, and it is a further piece of evidence to support our belief that molten metal was run into the grooves to form this type of decoration.

The mould for casting the pewter into the bobbin would most probably have been made in two parts of clay and fired to stone hardness to make it durable.

Lace tokens

During the 17th and 18th centuries there were times when there was an acute shortage of small change. When an enterprising tradesman decided to mint his own change in the form of a token others realised their usefulness and they too produced their own tokens. All types of tradesmen produced these tokens, grocers, haberdashers, bakers and of course lace dealers.

In the 17th century James Brierley, a lace dealer in Olney, produced a token. On one side of this token was his name and the letters B.I.M. and "of Olney 1658" on the other.

Peter Reynolds, another lace dealer, from Buckingham produced a token. He had his name struck on one side with a representation of lace in the middle of the coin and "of Buckingham 58 PFR" on the reverse.

Examples of the more familiar 18th century tokens are shown in the photograph. The first shows a seated lacemaker with the words "Lace manufactory" above her head. On the reverse is a sheep and the words "pay at Leighton, Berkhamsted or London" and the date 1794. On the edge of the coin can be seen the faint wording "Chambers Langston Hall & Co". This firm were wholesale haberdashers at 46, Gutter Lane, London.

The second token again shows a seated lacemaker with the words "Lace manufactory" around her and the date 1795. On the reverse is a scroll with the words " Muslins Irish Cloth Hose & c" and about its perimeter "Mooren 116 Great Portland Street". Both of these 18th century tokens are 30 mm (1 3/16 inch) diameter.

We are not sure whether the octagonal piece is a token or an advertising coin. On one side it states "Hall and Allan" with "Waterloo House 69 to 71 St Paul's

◀ *Fig. 31.1. Two lace tokens and a third octagonal token.(?)*

▼ *Fig. 31.2. Reverse of the lace tokens.*

▲ *Drawings of Obverse and Reverse of the 17th Century Reynolds Token. (Drawing by Robin Springett)*

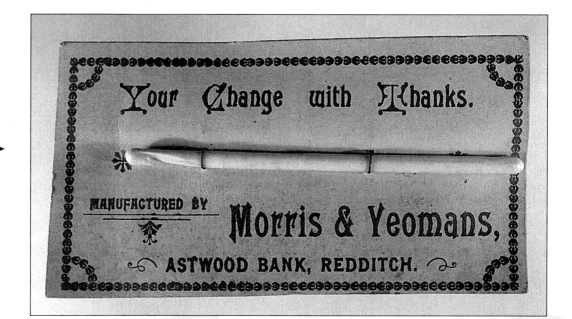

Fig. 31.3.
A crochet hook
as change.

Church Yard" around its perimeter. On the reverse "Hall and Allan Lacemen and Furriers" with "Drapers Silk Mercers, Haberdashers and Hosiers" in the middle

We understand that there were many other Lace tokens minted. Two 17th century tokens were issued at St Neots, Huntingdonshire, on one side of both were two lacemakers working one on each side of the same pillow, and "The Overseers of. Their Halfe Peny" on the other side.

Your change

Although this crochet hook on a card is not a lace token, it is a substitute for change. It was often the case that when lacemakers purchased goods from pedlars, lace dealers or

haberdashers they would be given goods instead of small change.

One modern day lacemaker told us that her aunt, (who died at the age of 80 in 1926) was a ladies' maid to landed gentry in Bedfordshire. When asked to purchase goods at the local shop she remembers being given a bobbin if it were 1/2d or a card of pins if it were 1/4d instead of change.

Bronze plaquette

This delightful bronze plaquette measuring 68 mm (2 11/16 inch) by 45 mm (1 3/4 inch) shows a seated lacemaker on the reverse. It was made in 1907 by Pierre Dautel.

▲ *Fig. 31.4. Front of bronze plaquette.*

Fig. 31.5. Reverse of bronze plaquette and lace token ➤
alongside to show the size of the plaquette.

Caveat Emptor

Fig. 32.1. Fake hanging bobbin. ➤

Fortunately lace bobbin collectors have not, until quite recently, had to suffer the problem of reproductions, fakes and forgeries, and even now the problem is quite small.

The hanging bobbin in the photograph is a fake and was bought at auction for several hundred pounds. We were convinced that it was not a genuine nineteenth century bobbin for the following reasons:-

1. The head and tail shape bears no resemblance to the work of any bobbin maker producing bobbins around the 1860's.

2. The inscription reads "Franz Muller Hung 1864 At Newgate". This is one of the most unusual hanging bobbins and none of the few genuine Franz Muller bobbins include "At Newgate" in the inscription. In fact none of the many genuine hanging bobbins which we have seen bear details of the place of execution.

3. The lettering does not have the 19th century quality because:-

   (A) It lacks serifs.

   (B) There is a larger capital F for Franz and M for Muller. On antique inscribed bobbins all of the lettering is of the same height.

   (C) The dots forming the letters are much larger than those on genuine bobbins made in the 19th century. Also the dots show no sign of wear from use.

4. The bobbin itself shows no signs of wear on the body, the head or around the spangle hole, which is as sharp, round and new as the day it was recently drilled. It may be argued that the bobbin was special and stored in the bobbin box and therefore not used, but it must be realised that these bobbins were working tools and this inscription was of no more importance than any other. It is only over the past twenty years that these hanging bobbins have been treated as special.

5. The "all over" grime on the bobbin shows an attempt to artificially "age" the surface for even the neck has the same colouration, this area should be lighter as it would have been protected by thread. The bobbin has the appearance of being fully covered, immersed or buried in a darkening material rather than having the genuine "dirt of ages" which is usually less evenly spread over a bobbin's surface.

Having studied this bobbin now look at an inscribed bobbin made by Bobbin Brown or James Compton in the 1860's, compare the quality and you will see the difference for yourself. Fortunately few lace bobbins command the sort of high prices that would make them an attractive proposition to an unscrupulous bobbin maker. However if you are interested in purchasing some of the more well

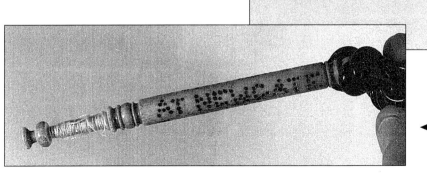

▲ *Fig. 32.2 & 32.3. Above and left.*
◄ *Two more views of the fake hanging bobbin.*

known collectable inscriptions it's worth taking a good hard look at the bobbin before you buy.

On the 14th April 1990 the following article appeared in "The Independent" newspaper. We are grateful to that newspaper for allowing us to reproduce the article and to Roger Bamber, the photographer, for allowing us to use his photographs which accompanied that article. Read it carefully for it speaks for itself.

"When is a fake not a fake? John Windsor meets an antique restorer from Sussex and unravels the mystery behind a recent cause celebre.

A Compost Of Bone & Old Lace Bobbins

In January of this year, 23 lace bobbins of the sort riffled through by lacemakers, appeared on the cover of the Christie's catalogue for a costume and textiles sale at its South Kensington auction rooms.

They were undated in the catalogue and carried estimates of up to £150 each, only to be withdrawn at the last minute amid cries of "fake". Some pre-sale viewers denounced them as plastic and there has since been recrimination in the trade press. Christie's would-be vendor is still unable to find a buyer.

John Carter and his son, also John 19, antiques restorers of exceptional skill and diligence, had sold the bobbins for an average of £38 each at a Graves and Pilcher auction in Hove.

Mr Carter vouches for their provenance. He says they were made in the 1920's for E. P. Rose and Son, a Bedford haberdashers taken over by Debenhams in the 1940's. He has a trade sheet from the shop which advertises ordinary bobbins at 5s a gross and 'Ancient Wood and Bone Bobbins.' He says the Christie's bobbins were among 1,000 E.P. Rose samples he bought from a Bedford woman about 20 years ago.

In the Carters' Sussex garden, a ripe-smelling compost heap contains the cannons (forelegs) and hooves of a shire horse, left there to rot and bleach for a year. Strong bone has been bred out of ordinary horses and cattle, says the elder Mr Carter. In any case, only bones of shire-horses are big enough for handles of the reproduction antique tools and lacemakers' bobbins which he and his son turn on a lathe.

Laid out on a table for inspection are a couple of dozen bone bobbins. Five are newly turned by Mr Carter as a test of his skill and are not for sale. They have ingrained grime, dulled colouring and a convincing nineteenth century patina. The rest, engraved with amatory rhymes, date from the 1920's and are from his E. P. Rose collection.

It is probable that the five home-made bobbins would pass through any sale without raising an eyebrow. Moreover, had Mr Carter senior devoted his restorer's skills to the 23 E.P. Rose bobbins before selling them, they would have sailed through in the same way. Even in today's fake-conscious climate, it is sometimes impossible to tell fake from genuine without proof of provenance.

In the case of the E.P. Rose bobbins, it seems that a little innocent forgery ("Ancient Wood and Bone Bobbins") has gone a long way. In this century, most lacemakers' bobbins have been mass produced. And the shop's bobbinmaker probably had no dark intention to deceive, in the Twenties, when he discovered a gift market for bobbins with the sort of saucy rhymes engraved by Victorian swains in the East Midlands. Whenever he engraved a new rhyme he kept a

▲ *Fig. 32.4. Mr Carter turning. (Photograph by courtesy Roger Bamber)*

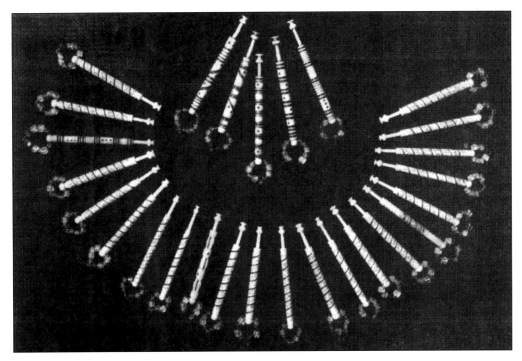

◄ *Fig. 32.5.*
Below is the heading which
accompanied the
photograph on the left.
"The Carters' collection: E.P.
Rose 1920s stock and (centre)
five lace bobbins made by
Mr Carter himself."
(Photograph by courtesy
Roger Bamber)

sample. Such as "To many springs have gone for we to waite to long" which was among those offered at Christie's.

It is just such rhymes on Victorian bobbins which have made them today's collectors' items. Some fetch more than £200. The Christie's specialist, Susan Mayor, before

withdrawing the bobbins following a complaint by Judy Wentworth, a dealer of The Antique Textile Company in Portland Road, West London, had thought they were late nineteenth century.

Ms Wentworth, a former scrimshaw dealer, was alerted by their even colours, lack of wear and uniformity – especially the spangles, the string of glass weights on the bobbin ends. The inscriptions were "too good to be true". She pronounced them "newly turned" and complained in the Antiques Trade Gazette of an "apparently deliberate attempt to deceive".

All of which did not please the would-be vendor, Corrie Fegan, a Brighton dealer, who had bought them at the Graves and Pilcher auction. "There was every attempt not to deceive," she said. "Christie's said they were wonderful".

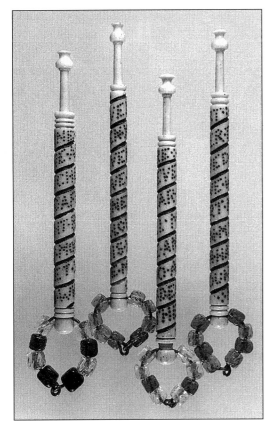

◄ *Fig. 32.6.*
Bobbins purchased in Cirencester.
See the next page for all the inscriptions.
Note the angle of each letter. Here each
vertical line is parallel to the side of the
bobbin shank. Bobbinmakers such as the
Comptons & Bobbin Brown formed the
uprights of their letters at right angles
to the spiral line.

Fig. 32.7. ►
Picture taken from
E.P. Rose catalogue. Note that these
spirally inscribed antique bobbins have
no turned decoration at the start or end
of the inscription unlike Mr Carter's
examples.

Ancient Wood and Bone Bobbins, with Antique Beads.
Name, Motto or Pewter Bound.
From **6d.** to **3/6** each.
Always a Good Selection.

Later, the Christie's letter explaining the withdrawal from auction said they had reason to believe that the bobbins were "only of recent manufacture".

In the matter of "fakes", Mr Carter feels that it is sometimes the dealers who lack scruples. He frequently sees his restored antique furniture snapped up at auction for suspiciously high prices.

For example, he purchased two 1930-1950 reproduction Victorian spoon-back nursing chairs, which he sold on without restoration. One, put into Julian Dawson of Lewes's six-weekly antiques auction, was recognised as a reproduction by the regular dealers and fetched £280, which Mr Carter reckons was its true value.

Three weeks ago, the other, which was damaged, was put into the same auctioneer's weekly modern furniture and effects auction, frequented by small stallholders and renters of shop space. It fetched £450 Someone, somewhere, will soon be offered it at an even higher price.

"It's not really a question of what is a fake but who is a fake. The fakes are the greedy, ignorant people who think they are being clever by buying the genuine article cheaply".

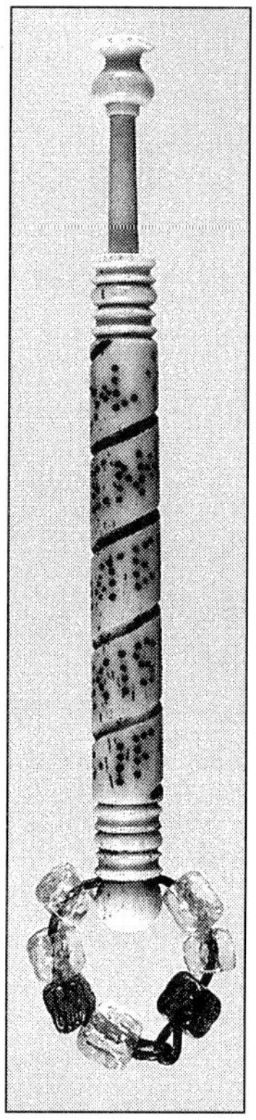

If demand is any indication of the real value of the bobbins that came up for sale at Christie's, then Mr Carter is perhaps in the best position to know their value. Up to five years ago, he was selling poorer bobbins from the E.P. Rose batch for £10 each at Brighton antiques fairs.

They should have been instantly recognisable as twentieth century he said. They lack a large glass "bottom bead" and carry too many words for an age lacking drills or engravers' power tools.

As to their quality, he said: "I wouldn't put my name to any of them. Any apprentice of mine who turned out work like that would go without wages."

◀ Fig. 32.8. A closer view of one of the "Cirencester" bobbins.

▼ From Fig 32.9 ~ A listing of those inscriptions, from left to right on the photograph.

(1). "If You Kiss And Tell Then Go To L."

(2). "Bedford Boys Is Best As Bedford Girl All Now."

(3). "Wish Well Wish For Me As I Do For You T S."

(4). "Make Me Your Bride And I Will Make You Happy With Love."

(5). " I Will Meet You By Moonlight But If Daffa Cotches Us We Are Done."

(6). "Love Me This Year Love Me Next Love Me Even When Your Vexed."

(7). "Tis The My Dear I Do Adore And Will My Dear For Ever More."

(8). "My Young Man Has Won My Hart Now We Will Wed Never To Part."

Unfortunately we were unable to obtain the original prints of Roger Bamber's photographs which accompany the above article. We have therefore had to use the original newspaper article to provide these reproductions.

Six years after this article was brought to our attention, a lacemaker approached us to ask our opinion of eight bone bobbins bearing spiral inscriptions. In February 1992 she had seen these eight bone bobbins at the Friday Antique Fair in the Corn Hall, Cirencester, Gloucestershire. The handwritten label with the bobbins read, "8 bone lace bobbins about 70 years old. Read spiral from bottom to top". She was rather suspicious as she felt that bobbins of this type were not made in the 1920's.

The stallholder was asking about £170 for the eight, having already reduced them from the original price of £200. The price continued to come down until £130 for the set was finally agreed upon. The lacemaker had noticed that the inscriptions were "a little too good", and that a poor head on one had been rubbed with a file and that they looked quite clean and unused. She decided that fake or not, they represented a lot of work and that even new ones would not be cheaper, so she sensibly accepted them for what they were.

Our opinion of the bobbins was that they were "of recent manufacture", but in this case the purchaser was aware of their probable age and was quite happy to negotiate what she felt to be a fair price, If another dealer had purchased them, believing them to be older, it might have been a different story.

▼ Fig. 32.9. Below. All eight "Cirencester" bobbins.

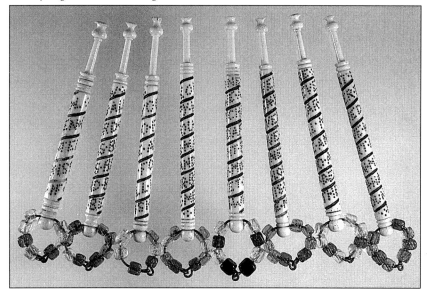

Heads And Tails

This section is for quick identification. For full details of the bobbins and their makers consult the appropriate section.

▲ *Fig. 33.1 & 33.2 The "Bitted" man. (Page 21)*

▲ *Fig. 33.3 Jesse Compton. (Page 24)*

▲ *Fig. 33.4 James Compton. (Page 27)*

▲ *Fig. 33.5 Joseph Haskins. (Page 32)*

▲ *Fig. 33.6 David Haskins. (Page 37)*

▲ *Fig. 33.7 Robert Haskins. (Page 40)*

▲ *Fig. 33.8 William (Bobbin) Brown. (Page 41)*

▲ *Fig. 33.9 Arthur Wright. (Page 46)*

▲ *Fig. 33.10 The "Blunt End" man. (Page 48)*

▲ *Fig. 33.13 Maker No. 1. (Page 55)*

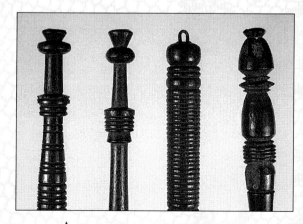

▲ *Fig. 33.11 & 33.12 Archibald Abbott. (Page 52)*

▲ *Fig. 33.14 Maker No. 2. (Page 56)*

▲ *Fig. 33.15 Maker No. 3. (Page 57)*

▲ *Fig. 33.16 Maker No. 4. (Page 58)*

▲ *Fig. 33.17 The Saunders Brothers. (Page 59)*

▲ *Fig. 33.18 ~ 1920 – 1930s (Page 67)*

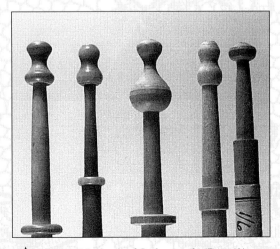

▲ *Fig. 33.19 J. Harris of Cockermouth. (Page 62)*

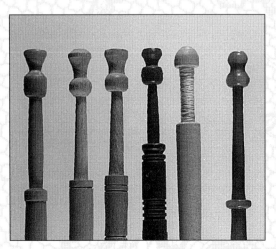

▲ *Fig. 33.20 E. P. Rose. (Page 64)*

Bibliography

"The Romance of the Lace Pillow"
    by T. Wright, first printed in 1919, reprinted by P. B. Minet 1971.

"Lace & Bobbins"
    by T. L. Huetson. David & Charles 1973.

"Pillow Lace And Bobbins"
    by J. Hopewell, Shire Albums No. 9. 1975.

"Dictionary Of Tools"
    by R. A. Salaman. George Allan & Unwin. 1975.

" Passenham – The History Of A Forest Village"
    by O. F. Brown & G. R. Roberts. Phillimore. 1973.

"Treen"
    by E. H. Pinto. Bell 1969.

"Dyes From Plants"
    by Seonard Robertson. Van Nostrand Renhold 1973.

"Textbook Of Wood Technology" 4th Edition,
    by A. J. Panshin & C.de Zeeuw.